# The Architecture of William Morgan

# The Architecture of

**University of Texas Press, Austin**

# WILLIAM MORGAN

## By Paul D. Spreiregen

## Foreword by Eduard F. Sekler

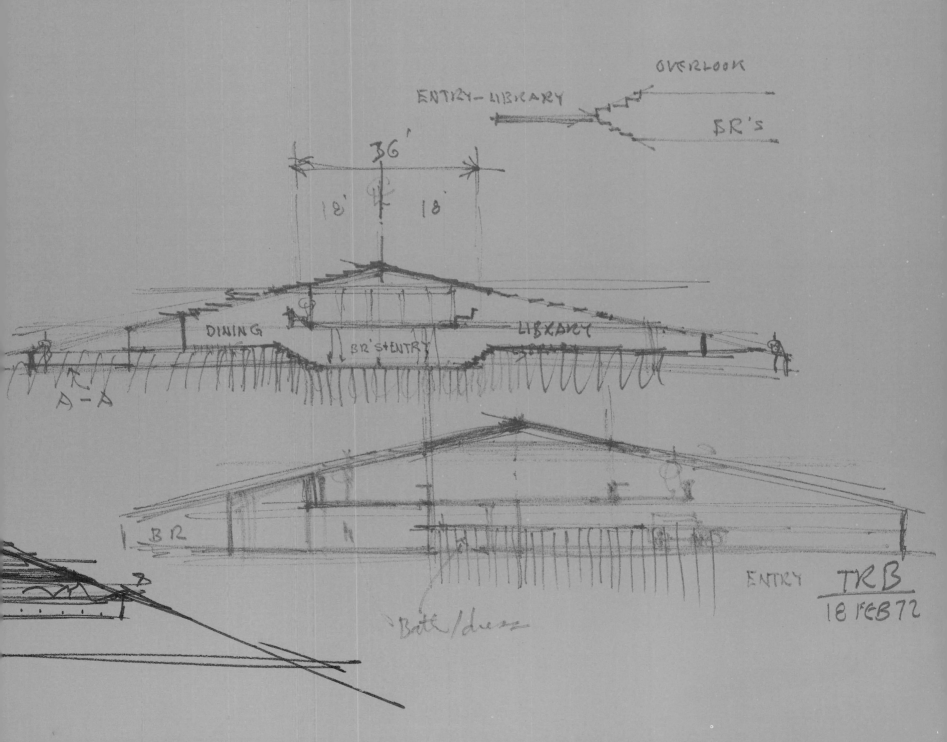

OVERLOOK

ENTRY—LIBRARY

BR's

36'

18'  18'

DINING

BR's+ENTRY

LIBRARY

A-A

BR

ENTRY TRB
18 FEB 72

Bath/dress

First Edition, 1987

Requests for permission to reproduce
material from this work should be sent to
Permissions, University of Texas Press,
Box 7819, Austin, Texas 78713-7819.

LIBRARY OF CONGRESS
CATALOGING-IN-PUBLICATION DATA
Spreiregen, Paul D.
  The architecture of William Morgan.
  Bibliography: p.
  Includes index.
  1. Morgan, William N.  2. Architecture—United
States.  3. Architecture, Modern—20th century—
United States.  I. Title.
NA737.M69S78  1987    720'.92'4    87-5983
ISBN 0-292-79023-6

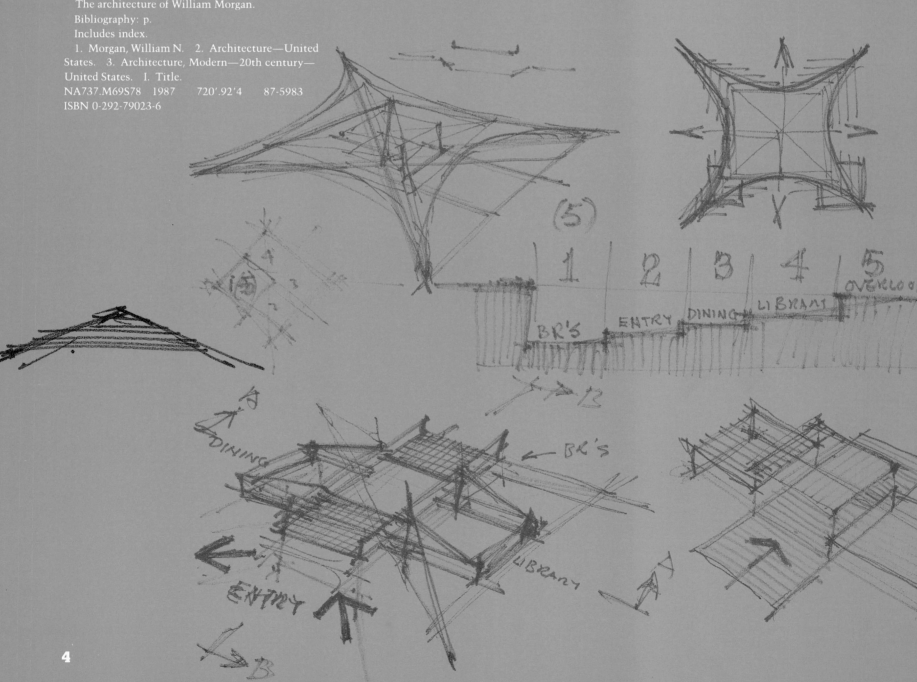

# CONTENTS

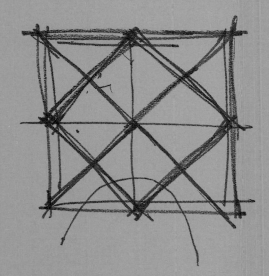

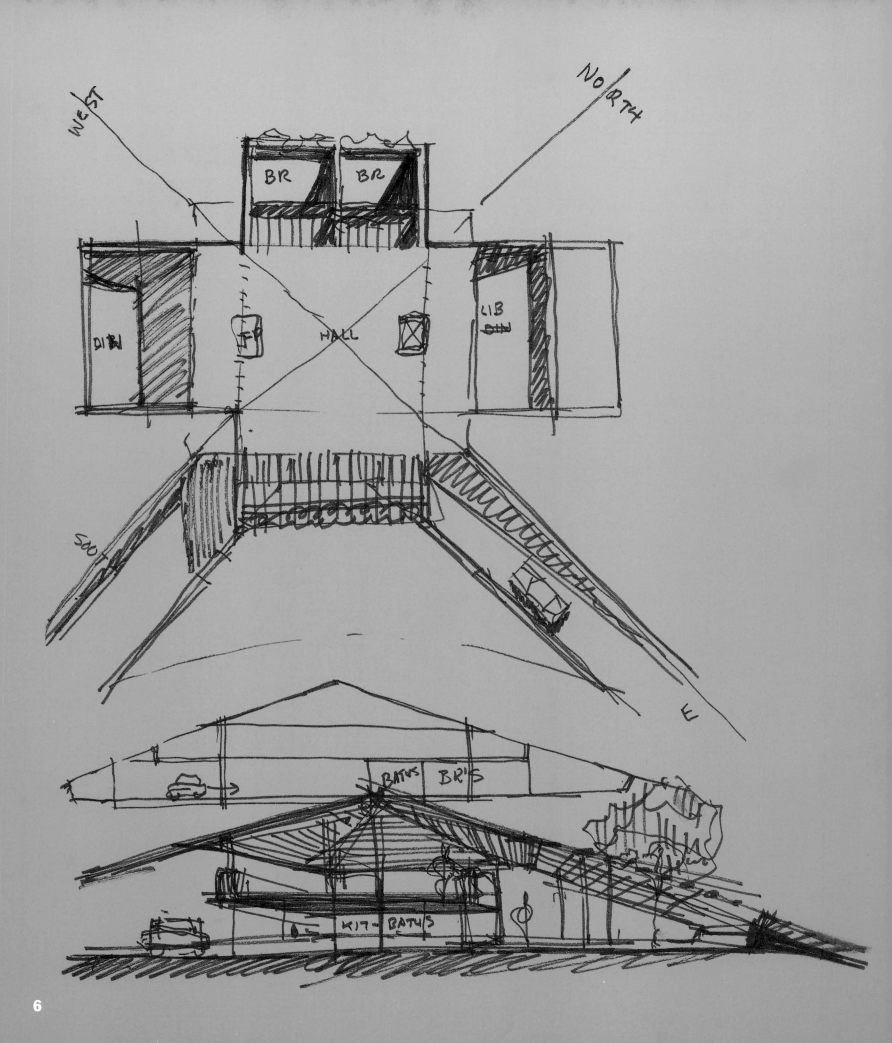

# FOREWORD

William Morgan's practice as an architect to date spans the quarter century from the early 1960s to the late 1980s, a period of profound questioning and searching for the architectural profession. He began to work at a time when the death of Frank Lloyd Wright and the dissolution of CIAM (Congrès internationaux d'architecture moderne) in 1959 heralded the end of an era. By 1969 all protagonists of that era—Le Corbusier, Gropius, Miës van der Rohe—were dead. Morgan, like other members of his generation, found himself faced with having to decide what, if anything, of the Modern Movement called for further development or for refutation, and where, in addition, one was to look for approaches that would make new beginnings possible.

As is well known, some architects at the time relied on technology as the chief source of inspiration; others tried by architectural means to render devices borrowed from philosophy, literary criticism, and other disciplines, and still others began to re-examine their attitude toward history. In the worst cases this led to direct transferences of forms from various periods and places; in the best cases the architecture of the past was questioned not for its forms but for its quintessence. One way of doing this was to remember that *principia* means beginnings as well as guiding precepts, and to search for principles by traversing history to the points of origin. Among these William Morgan was specially attracted to prehistoric monuments of the American Indians and, later, to the architecture of Micronesia. "Through this search for design origins in our past I am beginning to find meaningful possibilities for our future . . . ," Morgan once stated. The past, of course, is infinitely rich and complex, and one's selection of what to study in it indicates existing predispositions in the innermost layers of the creative self.

Morgan's choice happens to coincide with a prominent direction of twentieth-century thought. Ever since western artists first felt the impact of works of art from equatorial Africa and anthropologists began to explore ever more distant regions while archaeologists penetrated into deeper and deeper reaches of past civilizations, the workings of the "savage mind" and the recognition of archetypes have been the concern of leading thinkers, from C. G. Jung to Claude Lévi-Strauss.

In the past, works of art and architecture were authentic as they were in tune with and expressive of the highest spiritual and social goals of the culture that brought them forth. Today such unifying goals are much more elusive, if at all recognizable, and their place is taken by the much vaunted and perhaps equally elusive ideal of individual self-realization. Thus the artist is forced to rely entirely on his own spiritual resources, and authenticity becomes something very personal. In architecture it can become a destructive goal leading to works so idiosyncratic that their social value becomes doubtful. Architecture cannot be as self-referential as other art forms because it must be life-enhancing, whether it serves practical or symbolic ends. William Morgan's works invariably are characterized by the striving for this positive quality of life-enhancement. They may hark back across the remotest valleys of prehistory but at the same time they never arrogantly close themselves to contemporary life; rather they welcome and celebrate it in all its astounding complexity. Because they do so, they possess architectural variety which, however, never becomes chaotic since there is also a sense of unity, born from clear design concepts and from the necessities of economical construction.

Construction, to be architecturally effective, must find a convincing tectonic expression. The tectonics of gravity-bound bermed earthworks as William Morgan likes to use them, with their connotations of protective solidity and organic linkage to the maternal earth, differ fundamentally from the tectonics of the modular skeletal constructions he equally likes to employ, with their implications of lightness and aerial openness, enhanced by widely cantilevered overhangs. It is precisely the tension between these two contrasting tectonic systems that is one of the main sources of vitality in much of Morgan's architecture, and this is one of the reasons why the distant past of prehistory is of such special relevance for his work. Another reason has to do with the fact that the architecture of prehistory permits a tying back to deeply imbedded roots but rarely seduces into direct formal copying.

Prehistory, of course, is not the only period of interest to Morgan but in my opinion it is the most important one. Without its deeply moving lesson of directness and close linkage to nature and the land, he might have remained just one of the many capable architects whose talent, training, and competence enabled them to carry on and slightly modify the tradition of the Modern Movement. As it is, however, he was able to move beyond this level in a creative career that is still unfolding.

To judge from the achievements of the first twenty-five years, and considering that many twentieth-century architects lived longer than the seven decades traditionally alotted to man, there is every reason to expect many more outstanding works from the full maturity of William Morgan's second quarter century still ahead. As his prehistoric and historic references become more and more unselfconscious, fused with his concern for the well-being of his fellow human beings and with all the other design factors, he will continue to make artistic contributions of permanent value—permanent, because his architecture does not aim at the novelty of appearance produced by borrowing forms out of context. Instead it possesses the genuine newness of substance that stems from a reconciliation of past and present oriented toward the future in an attitude of confidence and helpfulness.

EDUARD F. SEKLER
*Harvard University*
*May 1987*

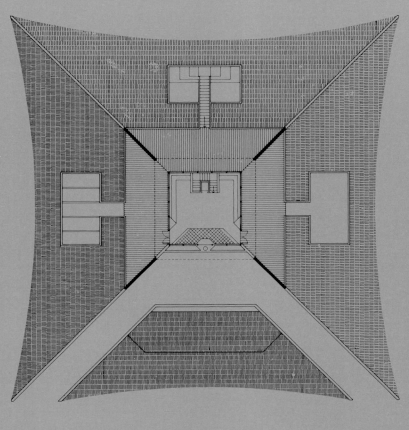

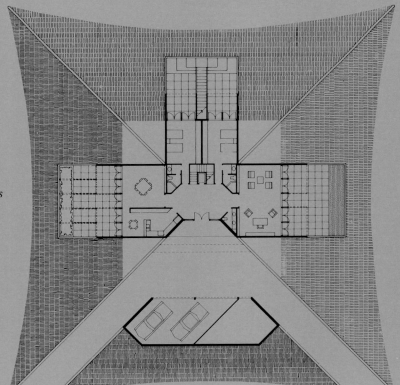

On the preceding pages can be found preliminary sketches that show the developmental stages in William Morgan's ideas for the Hilltop House (pp. 100–105), culminating in the plan as seen here.

# PREFACE

This book presents the work of an American architect over the past quarter century. Fifty projects exhibit certain tenets and possibilities of that interval. Of the fifty projects the predominant type of building is the private residence, constituting about 34 percent; 16 percent are multifamily residential. A third of the work is composed of office buildings, government buildings, commercial buildings, and museums. The remainder, 16 percent of the work, is composed of such varied types of buildings as medical facilities, conference centers, redevelopment planning, theaters, public utilities, and a church. At this writing the architect is working on the preliminary plans of a U.S. Embassy in Khartoum, Sudan. The variety of this work and the period in which it was done, together with the especially talented hand that produced it, stand as indicators of the state of architecture in America.

The author of the work, architect William Morgan, is from an area not previously known or particularly distinguished for its architecture or art. Significantly, it is in the area of his birth and part of his upbringing that he has done most of his work. Significant, too, is the era that informed his conscience, early childhood in the depression of the 1930s and the sudden sense of worldliness that the United States assumed as a result of World War II.

William Morgan studied at Harvard University, first as an undergraduate and then as a graduate student in architecture over an interrupted period of a decade, from 1948 to 1958. His education at Harvard came during one of that school's most fertile periods. Its modern outlook in architecture had had the firmest of foundations prior to the arrival of Walter Gropius. Under his leadership one of the most influential foundations of education in modern architecture was set forth. That was expanded, its directions branching, under the leadership of Gropius' successor, Josep Lluis Sert. With that branching came influential probes into the possibilities of landscape architecture as well as city and regional planning. Another formative influence was that of the architect Paul Rudolph, for whom Morgan worked while at Harvard. It was a fertile place to be, and Morgan was a student of that place at that time. The interruption to his decade at Harvard was a three-year stint in the U.S. Navy. That brought him to the Pacific and the Orient. In later travels he visited Italy and the Mediterranean, Spain and France, South America, again the Pacific, Southeast Asia, and Central and South America.

His practice reflects and draws on all these sources of experience and the disciplined view of architecture instilled in him at Harvard. Morgan's view of these sources, as reflected in his work, is the emulation of architecture's broadest principles, never its resulting forms. In this sense, his use of earth mounds can be seen as the utilization of an ancient and neglected architectural element, but for purposes derived from a specific design need. Morgan has pointed out that, while he believes that an understanding of design theory is necessary to creative growth in architecture, his own explorations have been in geographically broad areas of human experience. He has disdained imitations of past moments in Western architecture, preferring imagination to imitation, creativity to nostalgia, inspiration to repetition. Thus, his approach to history as a resource lies in the perception and extraction of architecture's fundamental relationships with its site, its climate, its culture, and its materials and, not the least, the internal dialogue that architecture ceaselessly maintains among its own constituent parts.

Such premises characterize much of the architecture of contemporary American experience. But, in recent years, these premises have come under question, even severe criticism. A particular criticism has been modern architecture's neglect of symbol and meaning as conveyed by its appearance, especially reference to the shapes and visual artifacts of Western architectural history. Indeed, at this writing, one of the most intense polemics in American architecture is taking place. It may possibly end with an enlargement of the American (not to mention worldwide) palette of architectural form, a more tolerant and pluralistic architecture. But it may, as easily, divert us from the higher premises of architecture in our time. Form, meaning, expression—all are unavoidably a condition of all architecture. Those aspects of architecture occur in all building. We ascribe meaning to forms in order to place them in cultural perspective. The question is not that those form elements of architecture are more or less valid or that expression and even reference to other times, places, experiences, or values are not a proper part of the architecture of any period. The question is the nature of their use, the intellectual discipline and design methodology that find form and then, finally, the expression of one's own special time and one's own special place through architecture. Successfully pursued, that may render the architecture generated by a certain place and moment universal.

That is the thesis of this book, and the reason for presenting the work of William Morgan at this time. We are at a moment of change, of questioning past premises and seeking new objectives. The much maligned architecture of the fifties, derogatorily termed "modernist," has become a symbol of all that seemed wrong with that period, and a basis for justifying architecture's present currents. It is a weak basis of argument. Seen fairly, the architecture of the thirties and then of the post–World War II period (through the late sixties) is properly appreciated as an architecture of discipline, integrity, social responsibility, economy, and technological application. That was its intent, if not always its fulfillment. That it was pursued within a succinct architectural palette had, as a fundamental purpose, the idea of making good building widely available, distributing opportunity to all, not a privileged few. Would that the same could be said about those currents in present-day design that would claim to be its successor.

This book seeks to confirm certain outlooks that have produced much that is of enduring value in architecture. It seeks to confirm the view that the continued pursuit of those values—enlarged upon with a sense of adventure coupled with social purpose—will lead us to the realization of great and enduring beauty in a special art.

# INTRODUCTION

William Morgan was born in Jacksonville, Florida, in 1930, the younger of two brothers. His father was a physician whose career was spent in the U.S. Public Health Service. The family's modest means in the depression years and his father's career destined him for considerable travel in his early years, first to residence in Brookline, Massachusetts, while his father attended the School of Public Health at Harvard University.

His earliest memories include the recollection of an off-shore cruise in a large sailboat. The fascinating and protective intricacies of the below-decks passageways and cabins, in contrast to the vast scale of the sea and sky, impressed him deeply. It is a relationship that came to underlie much of his architectural work. Family travels took him to Augusta, Georgia; Clearwater, Florida; and Falls Church, Virginia. He attended schools in all these places, the third and fourth grades in Virginia. His special recollection of childhood places, often in detail, was a beginning to his formulation as an architect.

The Spanish Civil War, the Japanese invasion of China, and the advent of World War II were all coincident with his enlarging childhood awareness. And so was the beginning of an interest in making things—carving wood, discovering a set of "blue-prints" at a house construction site, and building models of imaginary objects. His curiosity was constantly stimulated by frequent travels with his father.

His high school class had eighty-seven students, many more girls than boys, due to the war. Three high school summers were spent with his father, who had been assigned to a public health service post in Las Vegas, Nevada. From there he visited California and Arizona. Other western travels included visits to the great national parks and some of the great works of hydroengineering. The sight of Boulder Dam left a deep impression, as did the sight of the Golden Gate Bridge and San Francisco, the city canopied with antiaircraft barrage balloons. His last high school summer was spent working for a contractor specializing in poured-in-place concrete, which established a fundamental appreciation for the vicissitudes of real building.

Because he did well on his College Board entrance examinations, he received a Naval Reserve Officer Training Corps (NROTC) scholarship that enabled him to attend Harvard College, which he entered in 1948. His approach to Harvard was one of open curiosity, his first intention having been to study government. But that interest was quickly rivaled by interests in philosophy and literature. His first college summer was occupied with a Naval ROTC cruise aboard the mighty USS *Missouri* to Europe. Docking at Cherbourg, he was able to visit Mont-Saint-Michel and Chartres.

His sophomore adviser at Harvard was G. Holmes Perkins, then the head of the Department of City and Regional Planning in the Graduate School of Design. Compelled to pursue a field of concentration Morgan chose architecture. In one design studio, under the tutelage of Richard Filipowski, he designed a chair for which he obtained a patent. Walter Gropius was in the process of retiring at this time, his successor to be Josep Lluis Sert. Believing that some of the teachers whom he esteemed might be removed, Morgan led a protest in their behalf. A polite but firm reminder from the university that the new dean must have the prerogative to shape his own teaching staff quelled his ardor.

Graduated from Harvard in 1952, Morgan entered a three-year period of active duty in the U.S. Navy. The first nineteen months were spent aboard a destroyer in the Pacific, near North Korea and Formosa, all in relation to the Korean War. He served as operations and legal officer, as well as officer of the deck. He read the history of Japan and its architecture and visited several parts of Japan. He also visited Formosa and Hong Kong. His view of architecture was expanding through exposure to some of its classic accomplishments, as well as some of its most banal. But it was expanding.

In 1953 he was assigned to a seven-week program in naval justice in Newport, Rhode Island. His exposure to the possibilities of manipulating the law at the expense of justice discouraged any interest he might have had in that profession. His remaining naval service was spent on Guam, where he served as liaison officer with a group of civilian oceanographers. Their task was to install underwater sensors to monitor the world's first hydrogen bomb blast in 1954. While in Guam he met his wife, Bunny, then an art teacher for Micronesian Islanders and the families of U.S. forces living abroad. Their honeymoon was spent on the island of Tinian, where he first observed the ancient stone structures of long-vanished Pacific island civilizations. The extent of their accomplishments was confirmed to Morgan by a chance meeting with an aerial reconnaissance photographic pilot, who told of spotting canal and foundation systems on other islands. Later, teachers at the Harvard Graduate School of Design were to encourage him to pursue this interest.

One of his assignments on Guam was to meet the late Richard Neutra at the airport—and prevent him from visiting the island. Neutra had designed a number of buildings for the navy on Guam, as well as a master plan for the island. (The late Samuel B. Zisman, architect and planner and my uncle, was Neutra's planning consultant.) Because Neutra had gotten into a dispute with the navy, he and his wife were to pass through the airport but were not to visit the island. Painfully, Morgan explained all this to his "guest." Graciously, Neutra acquiesced. Morgan admired the work that Neutra had done on the island and gave him a set of slide photographs he had taken of those projects.

Looking ahead, Morgan decided that he would return to Harvard and attend the Graduate School of Design. With the educational benefits of the G.I. Bill in full effect, he enrolled at Harvard in the fall of 1955. Bunny took a job as an art teacher. Among Morgan's most influential teachers was the noted historian, the late Sigfried Gideon. Gideon's successor, Eduard Sekler, became a close friend and adviser. Another teacher was Joseph Zalewski, educated in Poland and later associated with the firm of Sert, Jackson and Associates. Still another was William Le Messurier, the distinguished structural engineer with whom Morgan was to collaborate in professional practice.

To help support himself and Bunny, Morgan worked part time in the Cambridge office of Paul Rudolph, at that time designing the Jewett Art Center at Wellesley, the Boston Blue Cross and Blue Shield Building, and the U.S. Embassy in Amman, Jordan. Serge Chermayeff, who had taught or would teach at Harvard, MIT, and Yale, had an adjoining office. Philip Johnson, then designing the Seagram Building in New York, visited from time to time.

But mother nature was to have greater influence on his student career. Wife Bunny was about to become a mother, her teaching career and breadwinning role about to undergo a pause. Morgan's finances were in a critical state. But rescue came in the form of Morgan being appointed a Lehman Fellow, and he was able to complete his studies. The first of two sons, Newton was born in 1956.

One of Morgan's student roles was to serve as chairman of the Graduate School of Design lecture committee. Visiting lecturers included Richard Neutra, George Nelson, Konrad Wachsman, and Arthur Drexler. Morgan also entered competitions, one for the Cowboy Hall of Fame in Oklahoma, his first essay in earth shaping in architecture. He also entered the competition for the Toronto City Hall, for which he teamed up with several classmates, including the Australian John Andrews. The team retained some of their instructors, including William Le Messurier, as unpaid consultants. The design was chosen as one of six finalists for the second stage of the competition. Morgan also recalls that Frank Lloyd Wright, in commenting on the competition's yield, described his team's design as resembling a "Babylonian brothel." To experience such appreciation early in one's architectural career can only add to one's preparation. But Sigfried Gideon, the then eminent historian of modern architecture, countered Wright's insulting quip with the remark that it reminded him of Borobudur in Java. That remark was to spark Morgan's interest in Southeast Asia and India.

Morgan was graduated from the Harvard graduate design program in 1958. His studies were capped by his being awarded the Appleton Prize for architectural study abroad as well as a Fulbright Fellowship to Italy. He spent much of his time in Italy attending lectures, one of which was given by Pier Luigi Nervi, the Italian reinforced concrete (ferro concrete) engineer. He recalls Nervi, in having to choose from one of several structural design possibilities, basing his decision on esthetic predilection—albeit a considerably informed one.

Morgan's travels took him through Italy and Sicily. He saw the work of the great and the not so great, the evidence of Western history's most fervent centuries. He found himself taken more by the imperfections of the Romanesque than the perfections of the Renaissance, stating a leaning more toward what might be possible than what had been accomplished. While studying in Italy, and as a result of working with the structural engineer Sergio Musmeci, an assistant of Nervi, Morgan conceived a design for a vast outdoor amphitheater covered by a tensile roof. The project was published by Zevi in his magazine, *l'Architettura.* As a result, some years later Morgan was commissioned to design the Interama project for Miami, which unfortunately was not built.

Morgan recalls his deep impressions upon visiting the work of Borromini, Brunelleschi, Guarini, Palladio, and Michelangelo. Of Michelangelo's work, he found that master's unrealized design to link Rome with great axial connections to be particularly appropriate, an early introduction to the harsh reality that not all of architecture's best hopes are destined to come to realization. Concerning the architectural work of Bernini and Alberti, his youthful eye found less to admire. The architectural historian-to-be Henry Millon directed him to the remains of Nero's Golden House alongside the Roman Forum. The great Roman baths and aqueducts were found without guides. The architectural evidence of the Etruscans impressed him with what he perceived as a special way of handling light in relation to excavated earth.

A fellow student, James Jarret, then at the American Academy, suggested that Morgan familiarize himself with the work and thoughts of Louis Kahn. In Greece, the first-hand observation of the Acropolis and Agora expanded his history book perception, as it does for all who come in the presence of those places. He found the Byzantine churches of Athens and traveled to Istanbul to experience, first hand, the expanding spatial bubblings of Hagia Sophia and the Sultan Ahmet Mosque. In visits to Sicily and southern Italy, he saw the colonial Greek temple in its many variations of siting and detailing, the great Norman Romanesque religious architecture of the crusaders, and the introduction of the Arab pointed arch, precursor of the Gothic in Europe.

A trip to southern France and Spain, as far south as Barcelona, presented him with French Romanesque architecture, Carcassonne, and Gaudí's personalized fantasies in stone. Travels in France culminated with the Gothic cathedrals, Chartres now for the second time but also Notre-Dame de Paris, Laon, and Rheims. En route he saw two major works of Le Corbusier, Unité d'Habitation in Marseilles and the chapel in Ronchamp. He found the light in the Ronchamp chapel of greater merit than the social intent of the Unité.

But it now was time to return home. Home was Jacksonville, Florida, where he worked as a draftsman for the architectural firm of Rey-

nolds, Smith, and Hills in 1959 and 1960. He obtained his license to practice architecture in Florida and began his practice in 1961.

As is the case in everyone's life, certain people at certain times proved to have a seminal influence. One was a young architect colleague in Jacksonville, Robert Ernest. Ernest had completed three major works before he died at the age of twenty-eight. His gift to Morgan was to convince him that great architecture need not depend on abundant budget. Great beauty could be achieved in a simple block wall, well proportioned, well positioned, its purposeful design given clear expression of intention.

Thus prepared, William Morgan embarked on his personal adventures of exploration. The results are presented here through fifty projects, organized into seven sections. At the conclusion of each is an essay—an "assessment" of the work itself, Morgan's related activities, and some observations. The first group of projects is, as would be expected, a flexing of skills, laying a foundation of capabilities.

*The following persons contributed
to the architectural development
of projects presented in this volume:*

Edgardo F. Agular
George Bull, Jr.
Perry Cofield
John W. Dyal
William P. J. Ebert
David Enghdal
Gonzalo I. Gaitan
Thor Heinrich
Sadia Kane
Keith M. Kelly
Dennis MacDonough
Linda Mack
John McCaffery
Thomas A. McCrary, Jr.
William T. Morris
Richard W. Pearson, Jr.
James E. Rink, Jr.
Harvey Schorr
Theodore C. Strader
Lynn Tenneck
Tri Vu
Robert D. Woolverton

ATLANTIC BEACH APARTMENTS

JAMES RESIDENCE

WILLIAMS RESIDENCE

RAWLS RESIDENCE

THE PLACE BY THE SEA

WILLIAMSON RESIDENCE

HATCHER RESIDENCE

1961–1965

## BUILDING

The building is based on the use of twelve 16' × 16' modules, eleven of which are enclosed, giving 3,072 sf of enclosed space for four units. The structure is concrete block bearing walls, on which rests a system of thirty-three folded plate plywood roof panels. These are set at a 45° angle to the plan module, forming 8' overhangs. The main floor is 4" above grade. The ceiling is 9'4" at its peak.

The building exterior is exposed concrete block, with natural cedar soffits. The blocks are plastered on the inside to reduce sound transmission. The location of kitchens and closets between units also contributes to the reduction of internal sound and heat transmission. Fenestration is in continuous panels, opening to terraces and draped to 6'8" for pri-

vacy. Above the windows, triangular clerestories admit even light, diffused by soffit
reflection.

## MECHANICAL
The heating and cooling system has a reverse
cycle heat pump, using water to cool the com-
pressor in both cycles.

## COST
Construction cost (1960–1961) was $29,280
for 3,072 sf of interior space, or $9.52/sf. Land
cost was $2,500. Landscaping, interior built-in
furnishings, draperies, and appliances cost
$2,150. Total project cost was $33,930.

# JAMES RESIDENCE

*Atlantic Beach, Florida, 1961–1962*

CLIENT: *Mr. and Mrs. Alvin D. James*
STRUCTURAL ENGINEER: *Haley W. Keister*
CONTRACTOR: *Charles J. Pyatt*

Many years ago the French architect Le Corbusier spoke of the box as having miraculous attributes. That remark does not sit comfortably in the minds of those who require that buildings present their eyes with rich visual fields. But both Le Corbusier and architecture's public are correct. The Parthenon is, after all, a box. Of course, it is more than that. It is a box only basically. It is a box with articulation, spatial hierarchy, structural expressionism, scale, optical correction—and so much more from Western architecture's palette.

Like the module and the all-sheltering roof, the box is one of architecture's great challenges. The "box" was one of the prevalent premises of the architecture of the fifties and sixties, almost a preoccupation. It may have taken that position because of the discipline it imposes. For that same reason it was a theme often pursued in schools. For house design the use of the box has a much simpler rationale—economy. The James residence may well be seen as an essay in all these areas of consideration—as one of architecture's persistent challenges in form, as an exercise in ingenuity, as an exploration in the possibilities in articulation, and, the most fundamental of all, as housing a family economically.

For all these reasons, this house is worth studying rather closely. Its seeming simplicity is deceptive.

## SITE

The site is rectangular, 200 yards west of the Atlantic Ocean. Topography precludes an ocean view. Setback requirements limited the buildable area of the site to a dimension of 22' × 52', which is quite close to its shape.

## BUILDING

The house was built for a family of five, including three girls, then ages 2, 5, and 8. The budget was modest. The two floors provide a total of 1,960 sf, including garage area and a storage structure and allowing for the open loft areas of the upper floor.

In addition to the garage, the ground floor has a central hall living area, kitchen, dining area, and family room. It also has a "powder room." The upper floor is divided by the living room—entrance loft space into a parents' side and a children's side. The concrete masonry units are composed of light beige South Carolina river stone aggregate. Exposed wood trim is stained a driftwood tone.

## MECHANICAL

The house is heated and cooled by a heat pump. It is mounted horizontally under the carport ceiling to save space. The ductwork runs under the loft balcony.

## COST

The cost was $15,867, or $8.62/sf (1961–1962), not including land, kitchen appliances, and architect's fee.

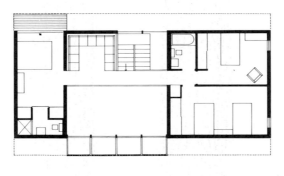

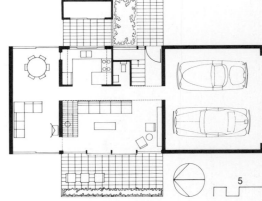

# WILLIAMS RESIDENCE
*Jacksonville Beach, Florida, 1962–1964*

In addition to being a rather fascinating design for a house, the Williams residence is an achievement in three of architecture's fundamental qualities. It achieves elegance, which is, to a large degree, a matter of understatement. It is highly logical in spatial arrangement, a matter of simultaneous separation and integration of functions. And, third, it is simple, which is a matter of resolution between all the elements constituting a building.

The client wished to have a house where parents and children could join in common living spaces but have needed privacy through spatial separation.

## SITE
The site has a southward view to a lagoon, with a panoramic view of distant savannahs. The house may be approached by boat from the water or by automobile from the north. The site dimensions are, roughly, 130' × 160'. Site area is about 20,000 sf, or just under a half acre.

## BUILDING
The overall form of the house is a rectangle, its interior a U shape of rooms around a central two-story screened swimming pool. The house has three interior levels. The lowest is made up of the playroom, pool, and carport. The middle level contains the principal living-dining areas, in addition to a bedroom and a utility room. The upper level has the children's bedroom and the parents' bedroom.

The overall dimensions of the house are 38' × 77'4". The roof slopes up to the south from 10'6" to 17'6". The main floor is 4'6" above grade.

## STRUCTURE
The structure is wood posts with 4" × 10" fir beams, 7' on-center. The lower floors are concrete slabs on grade; the upper, wood frame. Floor finish is carpeting. Finish materials include exposed concrete block, textured plywood, and insect screening.

## MECHANICAL
The air-conditioning system is a horizontal fuel oil furnace with cooling coils and a remote condenser.

## COST
The basic house cost $22,995 for 2,110 sf of climate-controlled interior space, 240 sf of carport and storage areas, and 360 sf of sheltered exterior balconies and terraces. On a prorated basis, this is $9.36 / sf. The swimming pool patio and the screened pool enclosure cost an additional $3,920. These costs exclude land, architect's fee, appliances, and furnishings. They include contractor's profit, interior carpeting, and site work.

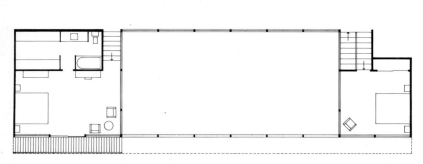

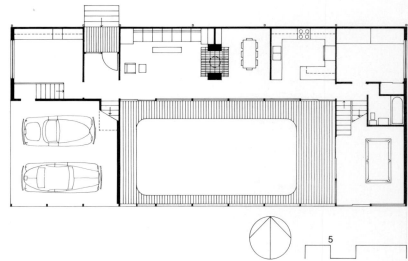

5

CLIENT: *Dr. and Mrs. Conrad L. Williams*
STRUCTURAL ENGINEER: *J. N. Hutchinson*
MECHANICAL AND ELECTRICAL ENGINEER:
*J. N. Sampson*
CONTRACTOR: *McCue Construction Co.*

# THE PLACE BY THE SEA

*Atlantic Beach, Florida, 1965–1966*

Morgan's largest early project was a mixed-use high-density residential development along the Atlantic Coast. As with his other projects, it can also be regarded as an essay into one of architecture's oldest challenges—reconciling formal order with complex intricacy. For high-density housing to be successful it must satisfy the dual and normally conflicting requirements of a rational overall form with personalized space.

The original program called for five principal elements—apartments, motels, common service structures containing restaurants and recreation, recreational open spaces, and parking. Specifically, the first phase (1966) called for 100 apartments, one, two, three, and four bedrooms. In addition there was to be a swimming pool. The second phase (1967) called for

48 motel rooms, 6 cabanas, 2 tennis courts, and about 50 garage spaces. The third phase (1968) called for 48 additional motel rooms, 10 cabanas, a 600' pier, a 120'-high tower bar, and a 16,000-sf beach club containing beach facilities, a restaurant, a bar, a rooftop banquet room, and a dancing terrace.

The design problem was not only to fit all of this onto a 7.7-acre site but, equally challenging, to be able to build it in phases. Only one of the major elements of this ambitious project was to be realized, the 100 apartments.

## SITE

The original site of 7.7 acres was to be developed in three increments. Phase 1 was to be 3.5 acres; phase 2, 1.7 acres; and phase 3, 2.5 acres. The 100-unit apartment would occupy

a rectangular portion of the site measuring 232' × 581', about 3 acres. The apartments would be located on the portion of the site farthest from the shore. To maintain easy access as well as view, the structures along the shore were to be arranged as five separate masses with ample spaces between them. The apartments were conceived as three stories high; the beach-front motel's units, two stories. Between the apartments and the beach-front structures would be a buffer of open space, part of which would have tennis courts. Parking areas, necessarily extensive and occupying much of the site surface, were laid out regularly to facilitate parking. They were also arranged in groups, with landscaped edges. There are a total of 200 parking spaces, 2 per unit. The building occupies 55 percent

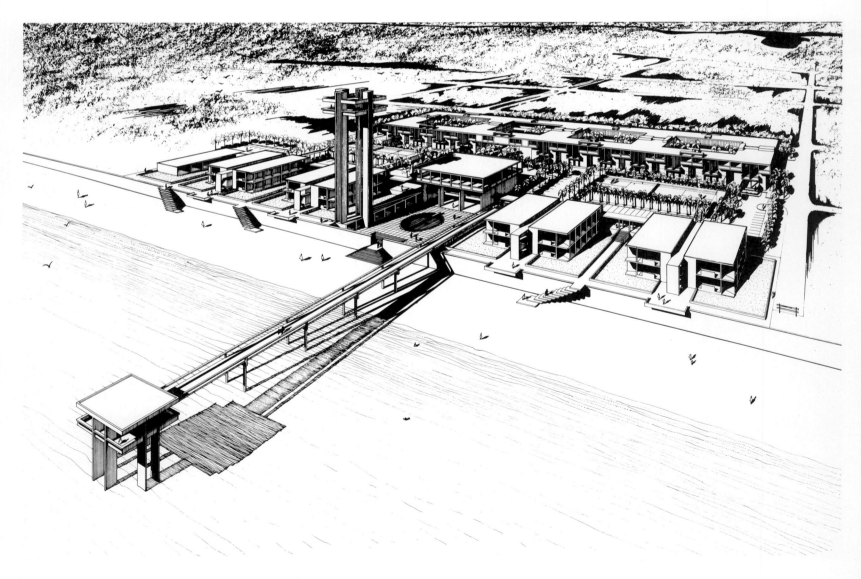

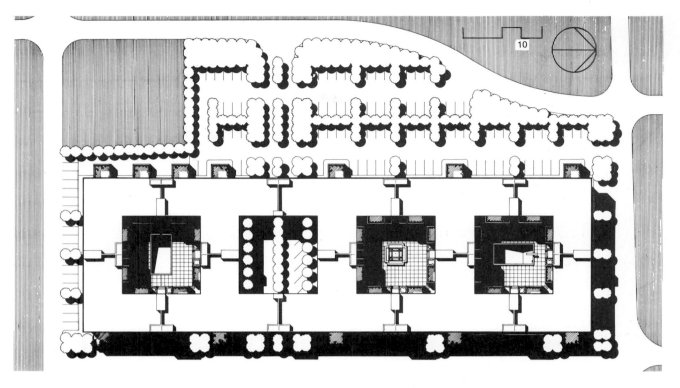

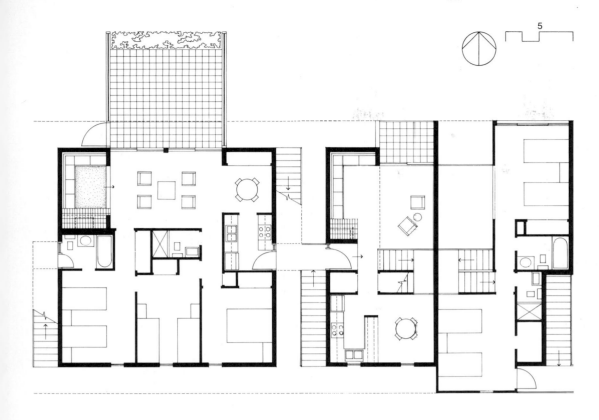

CLIENT: *James H. Winston and Hugh F. Culverhouse*
STRUCTURAL ENGINEER: *Haley W. Keister*
MECHANICAL AND ELECTRICAL ENGINEER:
*J. N. Sampson*
CONSULTANT ENGINEER: *Waitz and Frye*
LANDSCAPE ARCHITECT: *Frederic B. Stressau*
CONTRACTOR: *Preston H. Haskell*

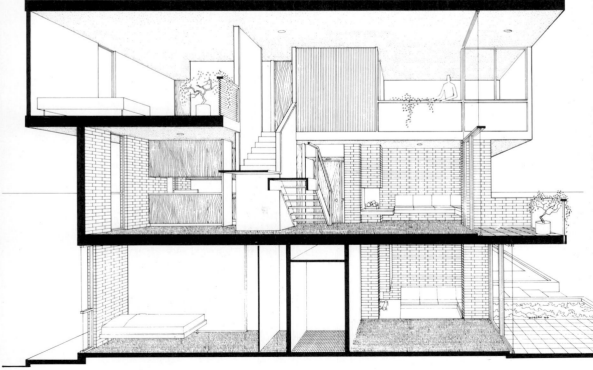

of the site. The site utilization density is approximately 30 units per acre, a density made possible by the proximity of the beach, the courtyards, and the fact that the building is one of a kind in a residential neighborhood of generally individual houses.

## BUILDING

The apartment structure is a single rectangular mass, measuring 160' × 520'. It is three stories high and is penetrated by four 80' × 80' courtyards. Three of these are landscaped, two with pools. One of the four courts is an entrance and parking court for automobiles and would have been a major access to the projected restaurant building. Most of the individual apartment units have their principal living areas facing the courtyards, with either ground-floor terraces or upper-floor balconies. Depending on the units, bedrooms face either the courts or the building's periphery. This courtyard arrangement has the further advantage of permitting through ventilation. Logically, the ground-floor units are the largest, usually having three bedrooms. These units have ground-level terraces and occupy a 40' × 40' module. Above them, typically, are two two-bedroom units. Each occupies half of the 40' × 40' module, each is two stories high, and each has a dramatic two-story loft in the living room. These units also have balconies. The units also have fireplaces in intimate sitting areas.

The gross area of the building, above grade, is 110,000 sf. The original monthly rental range was $175 to $300 per unit.

## STRUCTURE

The structure is quite conventional. Concrete brick bearing walls support wood-framed floors, portions of which are cantilevered. The natural beige brick is exposed and is waterproofed with clear silicone. Natural-finish cedar siding is used both inside and outside. Sound transmission through floors is reduced by a light-weight concrete fill on wood joists, covered with carpeting.

# WILLIAMSON RESIDENCE

*Ponte Vedra Beach, Florida, 1964–1966*

The Williamson residence is yet another architectural essay, again reconciling architectural formalism with the very demanding individual functional requirements of a family of six—four children and their parents.

The building presents itself as two assertive masonry piers, holding a long horizontal mass. This horizontal mass hovers above the ground, its sides in deep shade. The whole composition conveys a sense of joy with a sense of shelter, an apt architectural expression for a house.

### SITE

The site is a rectangle measuring 200' × 475', 95,000 sf, or a little more than 2 acres. Its long axis is oriented east-west. The site borders a beach along the Atlantic Ocean. The house sits midway in the site, its natural sand dunes and trees preserved. An S-shaped drive assures visual privacy from the busy highway on the west, Florida A1A.

### BUILDING

The client wished to preserve as much of the natural site as possible and have views of the beach, four bedrooms each with its own bath, a dining area with visual separation from the living area, the possibility of adding two bedrooms with baths, a two-car sheltered parking area, minimum maintenance, and protection from hurricanes.

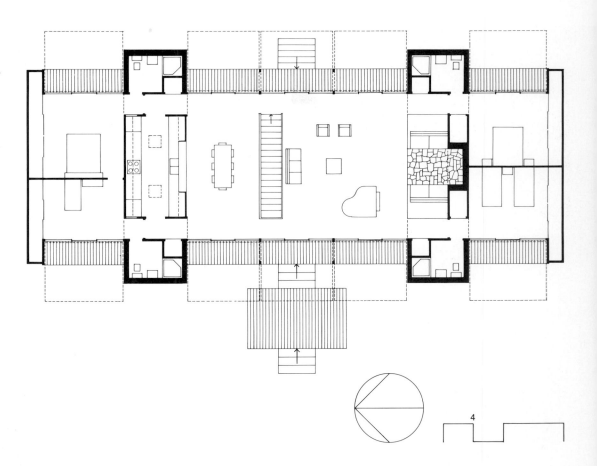

The house, in two levels, measures 30' × 78'4" at its upper level. The lower floor is below grade, the upper 3'6" above. Its overall height is 17'8", and it has 13'10" cantilevers at both ends. The upper floor contains 2,600 sf, the lower 1,560 sf. The open lower floor is convertible into two bedrooms with baths and a playroom. The equal emphasis of the two identical floor heights is countered by the partial siting in the dunes.

Pivoting sunscreens shade the house from sun and glare. They can be closed for protection against hurricanes.

The four masonry towers contain bathrooms and plumbing. Between one pair, on the upper level, is a kitchen; between the other pair is a sitting area with a fireplace.

This house, as an exercise in architectural form and space, reconciles two of the more nagging difficulties in design. One of these is the handling of the main entrance. The other is the position of the stair, also a major spatial penetration. The entrance is, perceptually, the shaded deck between the piers with the broad stair. This serves as a transition between inside and outside space. The interior stair separates the living room from the dining room, but it is positioned to form one side of the living room space. The ample size of the living room space also contributes to the sense of spatial repose.

The structural system is masonry piers, steel columns and main beams, and wood framing. The siding is cedar plywood.

MECHANICAL
The house is cooled by two air-conditioning units located in diagonally separate piers. Condenser units are in the piers, at roof level.

COST
The cost of the house, exclusive of land, landscaping, and appliances, was $40,000.

CLIENT: *Maj. and Mrs. Dan H. Williamson*
STRUCTURAL ENGINEER: *Haley W. Keister*
CONTRACTOR: *Ross Construction Co.*

# HATCHER RESIDENCE

*Jacksonville, Florida, 1965–1967*

One of the most ingenious and spatially rich of the architect's early houses is based on the spiral disposition of interior spaces, all contained within a cubical shell. The shell itself is recessed or penetrated on its four sides in varying ways to provide views, terraces, and shade.

The house was built for a family of four, who asked for a swimming pool with cabanas, a boathouse, and a separate study-guest suite.

## SITE
The site is on a tributary of the St. Johns River and is roughly rectangular, two sides bordered by water. The site measures about 130' × 230' and has a slope of almost 10' down to the water. To the maximum extent possible, on-site live oaks, some double the height of the house, were preserved. The house is located as deeply into the site as possible, still allowing room for a pool and deck and the boathouse and cabanas.

## BUILDING
The house, square in plan, is a compact 41'4" × 41'4". At the midpoint of each façade is a rough stone-faced tower. These contain utilities, services, baths, storage, fireplaces, a bar, and the landings of the stairway.

The house's spaces spiral upward, starting with a ground level containing sheltered parking, a playroom, a utility room, and a maid's room. The next level contains bedrooms, a serving room, a kitchen, and a dining room. The playroom of the level below extends upward to link with the children's bedroom spaces. The next, or "third," level has a living room and the parents' bedroom, dressing room, and bath. Here again space is linked vertically, this time the upper space of the dining room rises into the living room. The upper-most, or "fourth," level has a study, another bedroom and bath, and a terrace. A third vertical spatial penetration links the living room with this culminating level. The plan deserves careful study to fully appreciate its ingenuity.

The house's four levels constitute 4,060 sf of enclosed space and six terraces, which altogether comprise about 570 sf.

## STRUCTURE
In addition to the stone piers, the house is supported by 6" × 6" southern yellow pine posts; 6" × 12" beams rest on these. The floor structure is 2" × 4" edge grain pine used vertically and alternating with 2" × 3" spaces. These form a finely textured ceiling for the rooms they cover. Ceiling heights vary from 6'8" to 14'7", achieving dramatic spatial contrast. The stonework is a local light brown coquina rock. Siding is clear cypress.

## COST
The cost was $105,000, including the pool, boathouse, and cabanas.

CLIENT: *Mr. and Mrs. William K. Hatcher*
STRUCTURAL ENGINEER: *Haley W. Keister*
CONTRACTOR: *Ross Construction Co.*

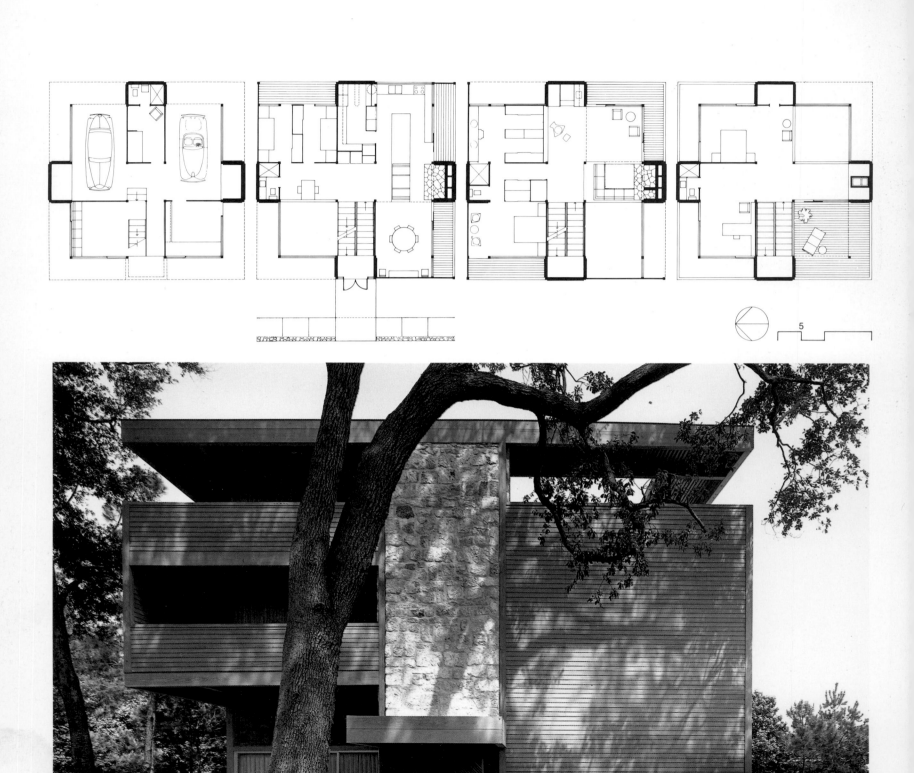

# ASSESSMENT

William Morgan's first years of practice were years of great personal duress. But they were also years of perseverance. The seven projects presented here represent the quality of his earliest essays. They are at the same time indications of his level of skill and precursors of what was yet to come.

The commissions were, for the most part, modest in nature, the Place by the Sea being considerably more substantial as a project. In all these works there is a striving for esthetic excellence, for formalistic and organizational perfection. There is a constant effort in behalf of achieving an almost crystalline clarity.

It is interesting to observe that this phase of Morgan's work is more often than not characterized by the use of symmetrical organization. Works of nature are as often symmetrical as asymmetrical. In nature, as one looks farther and farther into fine detail—more microscopically—the more exquisitely are nature's designs revealed. In the works of humans, the more microscopically one looks, the cruder a design becomes.

Such relationships do not escape architecture. In building design they most often reveal themselves in houses, which are, essentially, highly compact spatial compositions of quite disparate elements, elements whose sizes and shapes are not necessarily compatible. But architecture must make them so. Particularly resistant to integration in a house are entrances, stairs, baths, and utility elements. They have particular locational and dimensional demands.

Morgan's approach to this eternal problem was tempered by the design discipline instilled at Harvard and all but characterizing the architectural impulses of the fifties.

In the Atlantic Beach Apartments, for example, one sees an essay in the disciplining and repetitive use of a square module. The main element of the scheme is symmetrical but requires an asymmetrical appendage. The "umbrella" roof structure emphasizes the primacy of the organizing grid. Morgan refers to the design of the twelfth-century Church of Sant' Ambrogio in Milan, Italy, as a composition utilizing this conceptual system.

The James residence is an essay in combining two-story space with adjoining one-story spaces. In this work Morgan acknowledges the combination one-with-two stories of Le Corbusier's residential designs, such as the Maisons Montées a Sec (houses constructed of factory-made components), dating from 1939–1940. He also acknowledges Paul Rudolph's Umbrella House of 1954.

The Williams residence and the Rawls residence follow suit, the former reflecting the Weiss House of Louis Kahn (1949) and the Siegrist House of Paul Rudolph (1952), the latter finding precedent in the Villa Savoie of Le Corbusier (1929–1931).

The courtyard concept of the Place by the Sea has as a partial if not distant source the Lexington Terrace Apartments of Frank Lloyd Wright (1901–1909), as well as the Unité d'Habitation of Le Corbusier in Marseilles (1945).

The design of the Williamson residence was informed by the influential Richards Medical Research Building of Louis Kahn (1961) and the Cohen residence of Paul Rudolph (1952).

Finally, for this first series of designs, in the Hatcher residence Morgan found a parallel conceptual source in the Villa Rotunda of Palladio (1566). Of all the buildings, historic or contemporary, that informed his work, the Villa Rotunda is especially illuminating. It is a work of crystalline perfection, its proportions at all scales obeying the universal golden mean. It speaks to us in a language that elevates us. It is earth sited but not earth bound.

Palladio resolved those nagging insistences of entrance and stair and demanding servant elements by casting them into a wholly different realm. The Villa Rotunda, in plan, occupies an area of almost 12,650 sf. Of that about 7,000 sf consist of entrance steps and porticoes—well over half the area, 1.2 times the internal area of the house's first floor alone. Curiously, as Palladio gave primacy to entrance stair and portico on the exterior, his stairs (again four) on the interior are all but totally subdued. They are hidden in interior walls.

To a large extent, the architecture of any age is a new exploration into ancient and persistent questions. To see Morgan's "references" is to see him addressing these problems, recognizing their persistence in the work of others, present and long past.

This awareness, both conscious, and probably subconscious as well, was further informed in these years. Morgan was the recipient of a Wheelwright Fellowship from Harvard University. He used it to finance two trips abroad. The first was in 1964, during which he visited Central and South America, examining the work of the Aztec, Maya, and Inca civiliza-tions, with their many contributing cultures. The second was in 1966 and included visits to Japan, Cambodia, India, Iran, Jordan, and Egypt. The particular emphasis of these trips was architecture in relation to site, an interest that was to develop into Morgan's particular predilection, earth architecture.

INTERPOD

GOODLOE RESIDENCE

BALLENTINE RESIDENCE

JACKSONVILLE CHILDREN'S MUSEUM

FLORIDA STATE MUSEUM

STANLEY RESIDENCE

AMELIA ISLAND DUNEHOUSES

MORGAN RESIDENCE

1965 – 1971

# INTERPOD (project)

*1965*

Among the numerous challenges in architecture is to find ways of using the materials and means of one's own time and place. Modern times have witnessed methods of mass production and the almost constant introduction of new materials. Ours are also times of mobility.

In response, William Morgan conceived his Interpod project. A fully factory produced cube, 8′ × 8′ × 8′, was posed as a basic factory unit, with nearly complete built-in interior furnishings and fittings. With a few variations the cubes could be living rooms, bedrooms, kitchens or bathrooms, or storage units. As few as three or as many as six would constitute a dwelling unit.

Such dwellings could be installed individually in remote sites by helicopter. They would be grouped to form residential neighborhood clusters. They could be stacked, hung, or supported on vertical shelves to form high-density high-rise towers. They could be mobile units traveling on the ground by tractor truck, on the water by small boat or large ship, and in the air by blimp or airplane.

In fact, the ubiquitous "trailer" or "mobile home" is in its plan form as well as the fabrication of its components as close as we come to Morgan's notion. Mobile home assembly, as a rationally organized process, can also be said to be close. But that system produces individual models rather than combinable modules. And their use is restricted to land. They are mobile only in the sense that they can be transported from plant to site as whole units.

As further examples, one finds systems for highly specialized habitation, such as an Antarctic research station. Israeli concrete housing, using mobile formwork, also comes to mind in reflecting on these possibilities, as does the Habitat 67 structure of the 1967 Montreal Expo 67.

## STRUCTURE

Typical pods were to be 8′ × 8′ × 8′ cubes, aluminum shell exteriors with inner plywood shell finish, the two separated by 2″ foam insulation. Carpeting and large furniture would be built in. The walls would be prewired for electronics. Food would be stored in special units. Beds would convert to couches. Sun and light penetration through windows would be regulated by a variable electric current. Temperature and air conditioning would be controlled automatically.

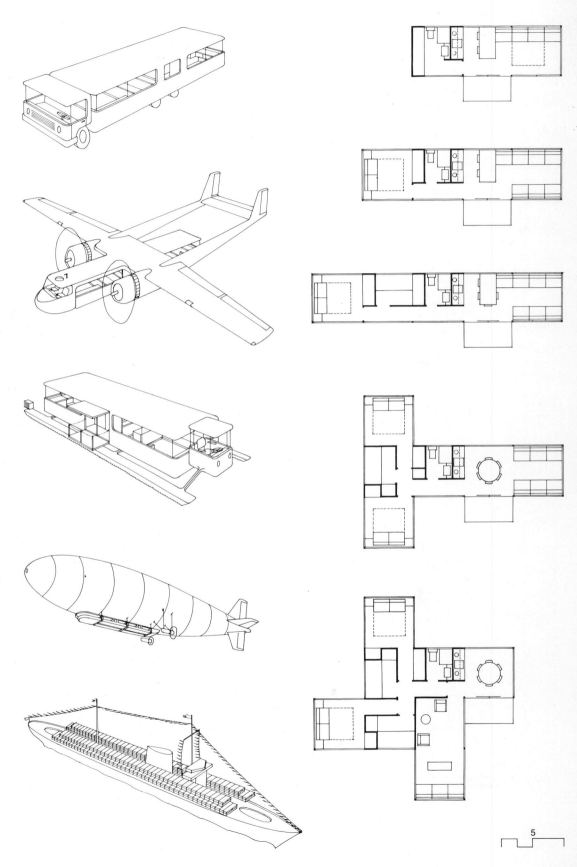

5

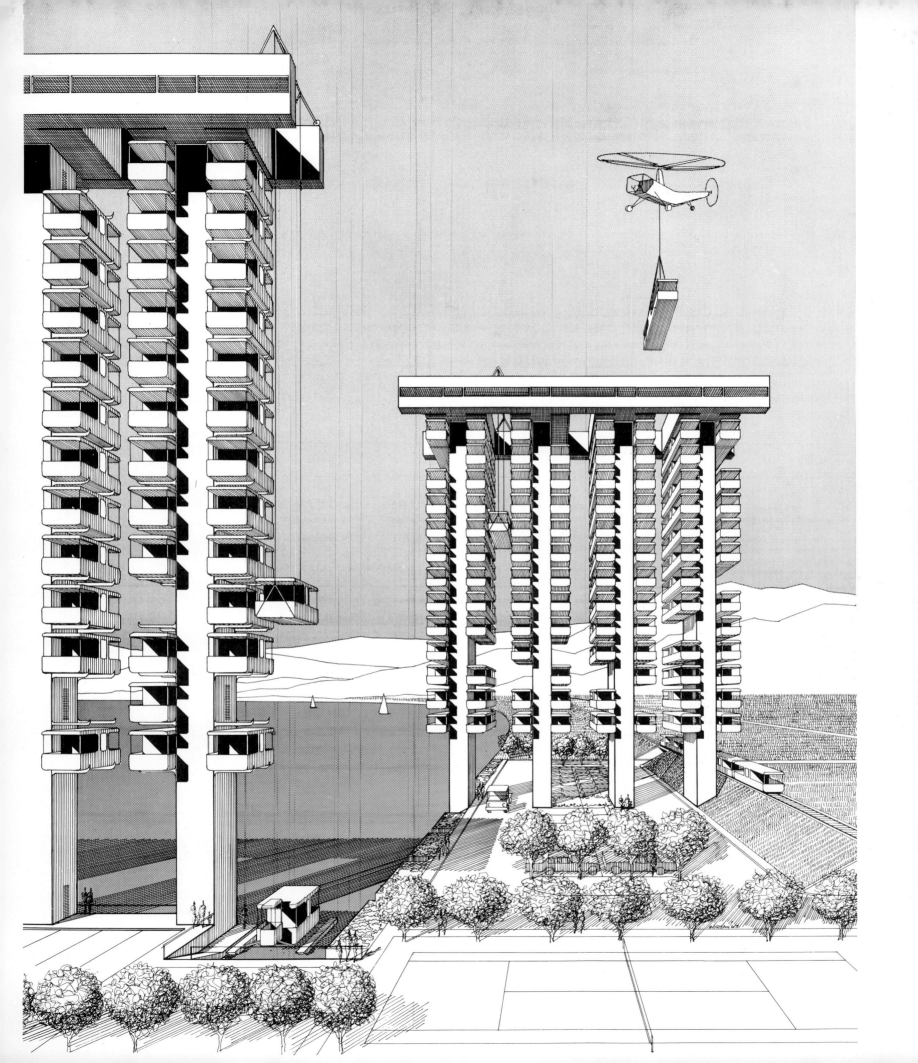

# GOODLOE RESIDENCE

*Ponte Vedra Beach, Florida, 1965*

In many ways this house is an application of the concept of Interpod. It is comprised of identically sized units, the units are stacked (arranged as a pinwheel), and the construction is innovative.

### SITE
The site is along the Atlantic seashore, with an eastward view of the ocean. It measures 100′ × 230′.

### STRUCTURE
Sixteen cast-in-place concrete piers support two upper stories of eight identical boxlike units. Each of these is 8′ high, 12′ wide, and 25′ × 4″ in a pinwheel pattern. The structure is conventional, built of 2 × 4s with plywood sheathing. This was covered with fiber glass—reinforced resin sprayed on in strands, a process used in constructing boat hulls. The siding is extremely strong for its weight and resists salt water corrosion as well as deterioration due to sun rays. A crushed marble finish imparted final texture and tone.

The house has 2,075 sf of enclosed living space, two large decks, two balconies, and the open carport and beach paraphernalia space underneath.

### COST
The cost of the house was $37,000.

CLIENT: *Mr. and Mrs. George M. Goodloe*
STRUCTURAL ENGINEER: *Haley W. Keister*

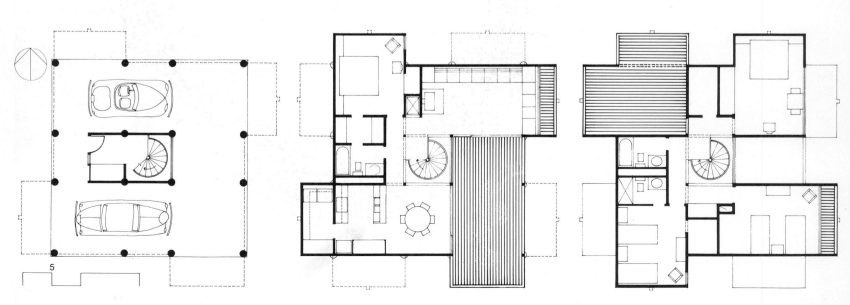

# BALLENTINE RESIDENCE

*Atlantic Beach, Florida, 1966–1967*

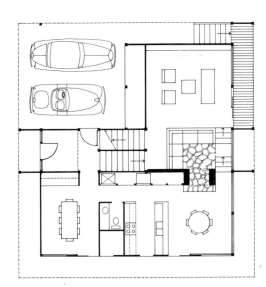
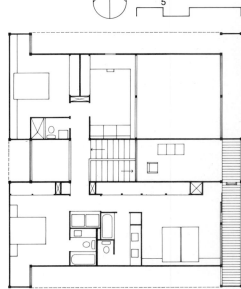

A characteristic of Morgan's work is the achievement of spatial diversity as well as continuity within a very simple geometric shell. The Ballentine residence, set in a densely wooded site in northeast Florida and about a half mile from the Atlantic Ocean, has four interior levels and a higher roof deck. The variety of levels is emphasized by four different interior ceiling heights: 6'8" under the bridge in the halls, 7'4" in the family room, 12' in the living room, and 16' in the entrance foyer.

The house contains 2,300 sf of interior space, 1,072 sf of sheltered space, and 1,024 cubic feet of storage space under the living room.

SITE
The site measures 150′ × 200′, set in a 100′ × 100′ clearing.

STRUCTURE
The house is a 44′ × 48′ rectangle. Its overall height is 17′6″. The main floor is 4′ above grade. Construction is post and beam, southern yellow pine, with exposed tongue-and-groove floor and roof decking. Exterior walls are rough-sawn fir plywood lap siding with preservative stain. The exposed beam ceilings contain room lighting panels.

The roofing is built up, over rigid insulation—except for the sun deck, which is neoprene.

COST
Cost was $35,000.

CLIENT: *Mr. and Mrs. Alan Ballentine*
CONTRACTOR: *Ross Construction Co.*

# JACKSONVILLE CHILDREN'S MUSEUM

*Jacksonville, Florida, 1968–1970*

The Jacksonville Children's Museum had extremely modest beginnings. Three local schoolteachers created science displays in the windows of a local bank, starting in the mid 1940s. In 1948 an old house became the museum's first permanent home, but it was located some distance from downtown. The present central city site is convenient to both residents and visitors alike—a corner site close to US 1 and Interstate 95, along the St. Johns River, and in a redevelopment area.

The original Children's Museum drew about 80,000 visitors a year. The new building was designed to be built in two stages, the first presented here and comprising 26,000 sf. It serves 150,000 children ages 5 to 17 annually. An additional 22,000 sf, planned as a second phase, is expected to double the annual number of visitors to 300,000.

The Museum operates as a nonprofit public service corporation. The city government and the Duval School System contribute operating funds so that admission is free. Among the largest early contributors was the Jacksonville Junior League. When opened, the museum presented exhibits in three major subject areas—arts, sciences, and history.

The highlight of the natural history exhibit was a 20'-long allosaur, reconstructed by the Museum of Comparative Zoology of Harvard University. Approximately one hundred live local birds and animals were displayed in simulated natural habitats. The technology exhibit featured the space explorations of NASA. The local history exhibits included local Indian artifacts, a prehistoric cave, depictions of Jacksonville's evolution, and a walk-through early-nineteenth-century country store.

To the maximum extent possible, all exhibits can be experienced "hands on" by the children. They can try on old children's clothes in the country store, climb into a space capsule, and operate the steering equipment of a ship. The museum also conducts a teaching program in pottery, drawing, painting, wildlife studies, and exploration. From the roof visitors have a panoramic view of the Jacksonville skyline and the St. Johns River.

The architectural organization for the museum is a visually bold four-story concrete box, its contrasting sunlighted surfaces and deep shadows clearly establishing its presence in its central area location. It asserts itself, attracting the interest of passersby, in a setting of considerable architectural competition. It is in an area of several far larger tower buildings.

The building's form is that of four sturdy tower structures supporting a central, elevated mass. Internally the central mass is open from basement to roof—four levels in all, the roof being a garden. The opening of the central mass has an open stair, from basement to the uppermost interior level (the third of the museum's four levels). The interior receives daylight from a skylight and from continuous ground-level glazing. Balconies within the central mass are used for display.

The towers at the corners of the central mass basically contain support activities and specialized functions—offices, classrooms, a 120-seat planetarium, a 150-seat theater, workshops, an aviary, an animal area, me-

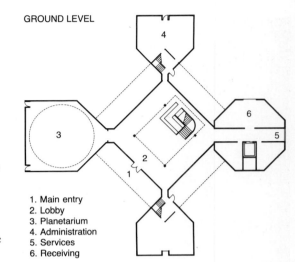

GROUND LEVEL

1. Main entry
2. Lobby
3. Planetarium
4. Administration
5. Services
6. Receiving

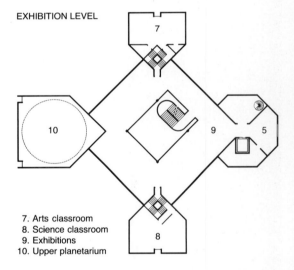

EXHIBITION LEVEL

7. Arts classroom
8. Science classroom
9. Exhibitions
10. Upper planetarium

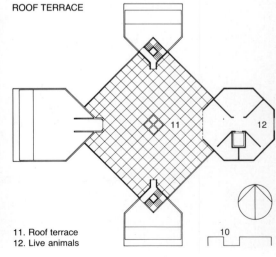

ROOF TERRACE

11. Roof terrace
12. Live animals

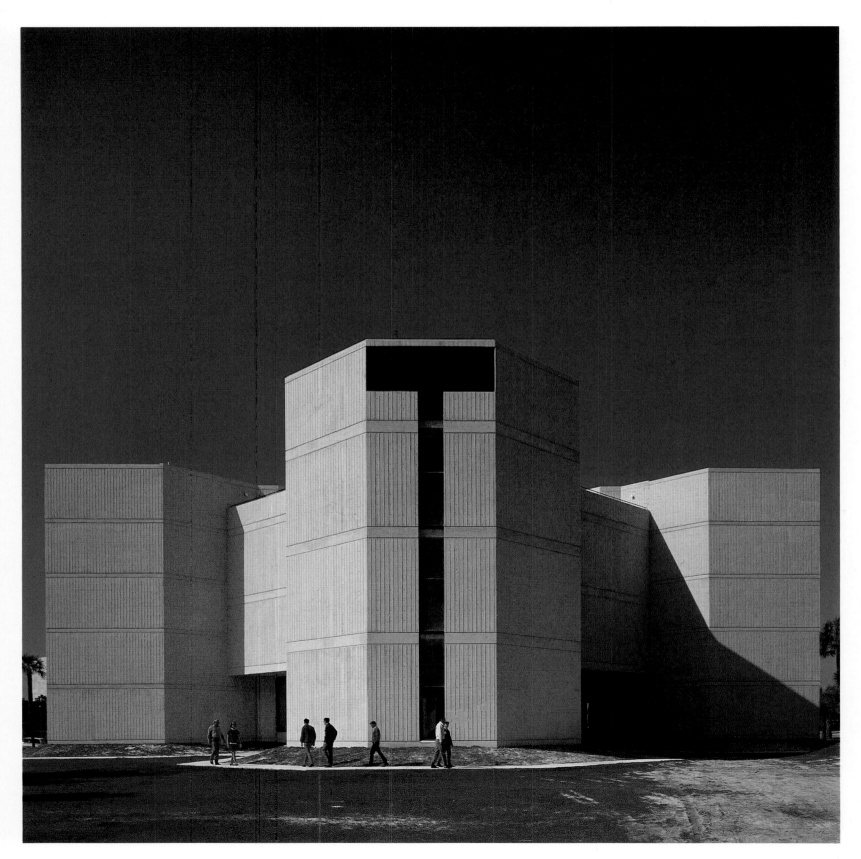

chanical rooms, stairs, elevators, toilets, and storage.

## SITE

The site is a portion of the St. Johns River Park and Marina. It provides a landscaped setting for the museum. A 3'-high berm elevates the structure above flood level and covers footing tops, which reduced excavation costs and eased soil compaction. This was more economical than using wood or concrete pilings.

## STRUCTURE

The structure is cast-in-place concrete load-bearing walls, columns, waffle floors, and flat-slab floors. There are four columns in the 72' square central space, which help support the 14"-thick waffle floors and roof. The tower floors span 42' and consist of 9"-thick flat slabs. Interior walls are gypsum board on metal studs. The inner surfaces of the concrete floors, ceilings, and walls are exposed.

## MECHANICAL

The building has a low heating load but a high cooling load. A two-pipe chilled water system is supplied by a 100-ton rooftop condenser. The chilled water is distributed horizontally along the perimeter of the roof to the four towers. Pipes descend into each tower to fan coil units in classrooms, gallery corners, and other service spaces. The units are contained under the slabs, above dropped ceilings. Fan units also contain electric strip heaters.

Gallery lighting is mounted on continuous tracks. Additional wall outlets and underfloor conduit 9' oc allow further flexibility. Classrooms and service areas have ceiling-mounted fluorescent lighting. The main lobby has spherical incandescent fixtures in alternate waffle slabs for night lighting.

## COST

The first stage of building, including 29,810 sf of gross interior sf, with an additional 9,275 sf of usable roof, cost $465,000. This does not include land, fees, planetarium equipment, and elevator. This amounted to $15.60 / sf, or $0.90 / cubic foot.

CLIENT: *Jacksonville Children's Museum*
STRUCTURAL ENGINEER: *Haley W. Keister*
MECHANICAL AND ELECTRICAL ENGINEER:
*Evans and Hammond, Inc.*
LANDSCAPE ARCHITECT: *Edward D. Stone, Jr.*
CONTRACTOR: *Daniel Construction Co.*

# FLORIDA STATE MUSEUM

*Gainesville, Florida, 1969–1971*

The Florida State Museum constitutes a major accomplishment in William Morgan's architectural development. It is his first realized work that integrates building and earth, a characteristic with which he was to become identified. It is also a museum of considerable interest from several other pertinent standpoints.

Established in 1917, the original museum occupied a 40,000-sf office building a mile from the University of Florida campus. The primary areas of interest are pre-Columbian Florida and the Caribbean. In function the museum is similar to the Smithsonian Institution, supporting research and public education. The museum collection includes 1 million vertebrate fossils, 200,000 mollusks, 100,000 fish, 50,000 fossils, 30,000 amphibi-

ans, 10,000 birds, and 7,000 mammals. The Pearsall Collection of Indian Artifacts includes over 400,000 objects. An 85 percent complete mammoth skeleton weighing 1,600 pounds was discovered by the museum's staff.

The new museum program was developed by its director, Dr. Joshua C. Dickinson, Jr. It was a most demanding program. A facility of 100,000 sf was described in detail, two-thirds for scientific research and one-third for public exhibit area. The budget was fixed at $21 / sf and construction was to be under way within twelve months. Allowing four months for review, administration, and bidding left only eight months for design and the preparation of working drawings.

There were five principal and simultaneous design requirements, in the architect's view.

First, the building had to be appropriate to its place and time and highly attractive to the community of students and faculty of the host university. Second, it had to function efficiently. Third, it had to be built within a strict and limited budget. Fourth, its design had to be approved by the National Science Foundation, the State of Florida Board of Regents, the Museum Trustees, the Museum director, and staff assistants. Fifth, all this had to be achieved within an overall twelve-month period.

The architect and Dr. Dickinson visited several facilities that contained examples of elements of the program. Museum books were consulted, among them *The New Museum*, by Michael Brawne. Among the museum prototypes studied were the Museum of History

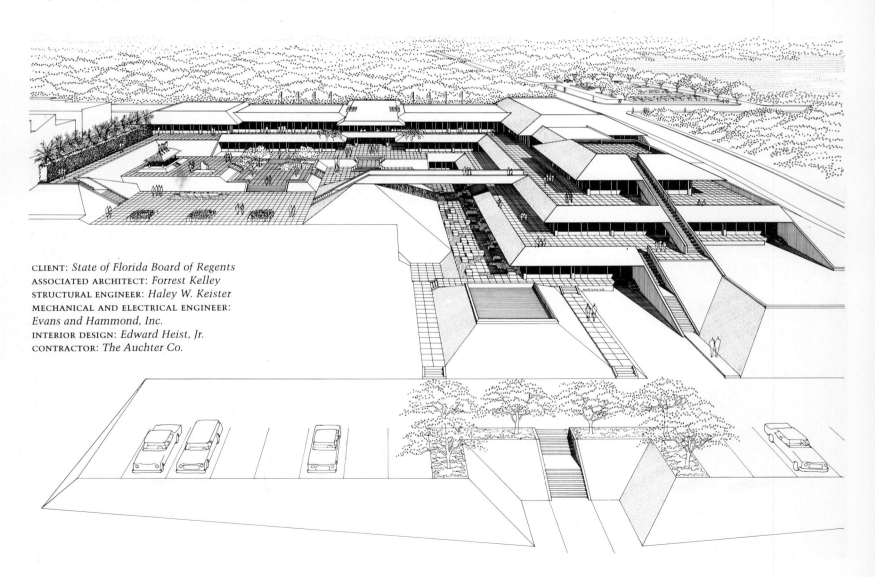

CLIENT: *State of Florida Board of Regents*
ASSOCIATED ARCHITECT: *Forrest Kelley*
STRUCTURAL ENGINEER: *Haley W. Keister*
MECHANICAL AND ELECTRICAL ENGINEER:
*Evans and Hammond, Inc.*
INTERIOR DESIGN: *Edward Heist, Jr.*
CONTRACTOR: *The Auchter Co.*

and Anthropology in Mexico City, designed by Pedro Ramírez Vasques, and the Oakland Museum, designed by Kevin Roche and John Dinkeloo. The various museum projects of Le Corbusier were also studied. The architect's visits to museums and sites in Italy, Peru, the Yucatán, Cambodia, India, and the Middle East were recalled. In the course of the work the architect met the archaeologist Ripley Bullen, among others. This stimulated his interest in the prehistoric earth architecture of the eastern United States.

Reflecting on all these sources of study and precedent, it became clear to Morgan that this museum was a unique opportunity. Its design would have to derive from the unique nature of the site, the climate, and the program. It is apparent, though, that the organizing form

concept of this building is as much a reference to pre-Columbian earth structures, a notion handily supported by the site's form and the building's function.

SITE
The site is a five-acre L-shaped area at the corner of two intersecting streets, near the center of the University of Florida campus. The open portion of the "el" faces southwest. The western edge of the site is bordered by an agricultural engineering building (to be transformed into a Gallery of Transportation and Machinery); the southern side, by a new seven-story biological sciences building. A grassy swale descends southward into a wooded valley. The two "arms" of the L-shaped site measure 265' × 445' and 120' × 215'.

A simple model of the site and its peripheral area was constructed to illustrate the nature of spaces, building masses, and pedestrian and vehicular movement routes. From that and the building program, the design concept emerged.

Staff parking is in several on-site levels. Public parking is on the campus, nearby.

STRUCTURE
There seemed to be three possibilities for the building design. First was a cube on the northeast corner of the site, with a court between it and two neighboring buildings. This posed obvious problems of separation of functions—public exhibit, nonpublic research, artifact storage, vertical transportation, expandability, and cost. Second was a building totally below-

ground. That idea was rejected because of difficulties of public access, lack of suitable "presence", servicing, cost, and not least, possible difficulties in obtaining approvals. The third and selected possibility was a terraced structure, descending the site's natural contours. This would allow an appropriate public entrance from a main street, burrowing portions of the structure into the earth, appropriate separation of functions, the creation of a series of terraced court spaces to adjoining buildings, and a good chance of an economic structure. Passenger as well as freight elevators would not be needed, since each level could have its own truck service dock. This would prove a major cost saving.

The uppermost floor presents itself as a one-story building on its northern side, which faces the center of the campus, and is the principal visitor entrance. Visitors can also enter from the terraced courts on the south. The uppermost floor, 34,000 sf, has a reception area, exhibit space, and administrative offices. All of its northern side and half of its eastern side are without windows, that exterior wall treated as a berm. Shaded glazing forms the south and west facing walls.

The middle level provides 45,000 sf for natural sciences research. Slightly more than half of that is occupied by research offices and workplaces, the remainder for storage. The northern and eastern sides of this floor are burrowed into the earth. That portion of the floor space is used for storage. The south and west facing walls are fenestrated, with views into the terraced courts.

The third and lowest level is used for the social sciences and contains 23,000 sf, again a little more than half for work, the remainder for storage. Its western side is glazed and has courtyard views.

The terraced courts themselves are composed of numerous levels in the form of truncated pyramids. They furnish numerous opportunities for outdoor exhibits. The terraces were designed so that they could have characteristic botanical specimens as well as archaeological reconstructions. They also invite pedestrian passage and have been used for a variety of student activities.

The characteristic form of the entire ensemble is a composition of reposeful horizontals, tied together by a pervasive 1:2 (1 vertical, 2 horizontal) angular slope. This slope commences in the earth berm, which forms the building's public perimeter along the two main streets. Its rationale is that the 1:2 ratio is a stable angle for earth mounding, often used in prehistoric earth-mounded constructions. The same angle is utilized in the concrete roof overhangs, in walkway pergolas, and on the sides of the courtyard terraces. All this allows unity and identity with variety. It also makes it possible for the building to have its own personality, which, at the same time, does not enter into visual competition with its surroundings. It stands on its own, a polite but self-assured neighbor.

Structurally, the building utilizes an almost commonplace construction technique—almost commonplace because a large part of the technique is used not for buildings but rather for highway construction. That, specifically, is the concrete wall and berm system that forms much of the exterior wall. The berm rises 10' above grade. The building is again as much below grade. Around 150,000 cubic feet of sandy soil was moved, using road-building earth-moving equipment. With the sloping site, the uppermost floor was at grade on the high part of the site, 10'6" above grade at the lower part of the site.

Structure is a combination of concrete slabs on grade, concrete "retaining walls," concrete waffle slab, cast-in-place concrete columns, and steel roof trusses. The (upper) exhibit floor is column free. Cantilevers extend 10'6". The concrete columns supporting the waffle slabs are 27' on center, both ways.

The 187 perimeter, or "brow," canopies serve as sun shades, rain protection, balustrades, and an architecturally unifying element. They were cast as hollow-core units—some 8" thick, some 3" thick. Their sizes range from 3' × 27' to 14' × 27'. Larger units were post tensioned.

A "Koppers" tar-saturated two-ply membrane was used on the foundation and as a layer between it and precast surface slabs. The same system was used on all below-grade walls and under traffic decks with 1" rigid insulation board. A four-ply system was used over concrete as well as metal deck areas; five-ply was used under a rooftop vivarium.

## MECHANICAL

Although designed before the 1974 energy crisis, the museum proved to be quite energy efficient. Even after electrical consumption was reduced, the required storage area temperature of 71°F was maintained within one degree. Reduction in electric light usage cut

daily consumption from 6,328 KWH to 5,157 KWH. Restricting air conditioning to twelve hours daily (7:00 A.M. to 7:00 P.M.) further reduced daily consumption to 3,537 KWH. By stopping air conditioning at 5:00, consumption was brought down to 3,315 KWH, a total 48 percent saving.

## COST

The original project budget was $2,100,000, or $21 / sf for 100,000 sf. A grant of more than $1,000,000 from the National Science Foundation and $800,000 from private sources helped pay for it. Final cost was $2,166,000 for 102,242 sf, or $21.19 / sf. Half of the construction cost was contributed by the NSF, 35 percent by private contributions, and 15 percent by the state.

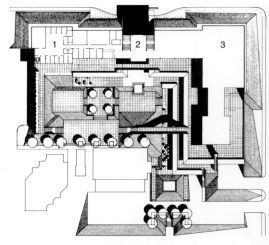

1. Staff
2. Reception
3. Exhibitions
4. Natural Sciences
5. Social Sciences

UPPER LEVEL—EXHIBITIONS

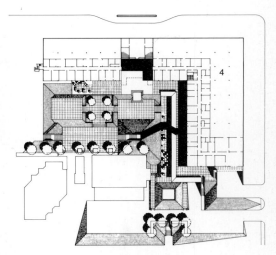

MIDDLE LEVEL—NATURAL SCIENCES

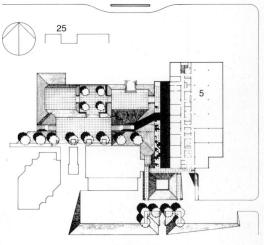

LOWER LEVEL—SOCIAL SCIENCES

# STANLEY RESIDENCE

*Gainesville, Florida, 1970–1971*

The designs of the Hatcher and Goodloe residences, both done about five years earlier, were essays in the use of ascending spatial spirals in pinwheel configuration. The Goodloe residence made use of a repeating architectural "box" increment. The Interpod project explored the full range of applications of the repeating "box," as well as the possibilities of industrialized building processes and materials.

All these interests are the basis of the design of the Stanley residence. And they all carried forward in a simple yet highly resolved manner. Four double-story "boxes" arranged in a pinwheel pattern ascend a quarter of a floor level (2'3") per "box." A central stair, with four risers per stair run, connects the levels. The whole ensemble is supported on nine treated-wood posts, which are clearly visible on the outside of the house, thus giving clear expression to the post-box composition.

The client was a professor of forestry at the University of Florida and a collector of art. The program called for a house with ample wall area for displaying graphic art, and sleeping areas for parents and two children.

The house is entered by means of a ramp that leads into a two-story screened porch (one of the four "boxes"); from there the ramp goes to the main entrance, which is a portion of the central spiral stair. All interior circulation is handled on this stair, achieving a high degree of spatial efficiency.

The sequence of major interior spaces begins with the living room, continues with a recreation or family room, and then proceeds to the kitchen-dining area. The living room and dining room have eastward water views. The living room has three unbroken walls for displaying art as well as for bookshelves. Continuing upward, one next arrives at a studio-study, the two children's bedrooms, and the parents' bedroom (with bath and dressing area). The parents' bedroom also has a water view.

The overall "logic" of that design could not be more reasonable or more simple. Yet the variety of spatial experiences could not be greater. The "boxes" are a modest 16' wide and 24' long. The house's overall dimensions are a square, 34'8" on a side.

## SITE

The site is 53' wide and 200' long, a quarter acre. The site slopes down to a lake on its eastern edge. Sheltered parking is under the living room "box."

## STRUCTURE

The nine support piers are made of treated southern yellow pine set in concrete cylinders to a depth of 10'. Their irregularities in diameter are compensated for by connection washers, which permit 2" of adjustment at beam connections. Beams are held against the posts by means of double bolts and a specially designed shear-friction plate.

Floors are factory laminated edge grain pine, forming 12"-wide planks in an unbroken span. Floors and ceilings are exposed wood. This type of construction, used for flat-bed truck bottoms, resembles a bowling alley surface when finished. Walls are rough-sawn fir plywood horizontally lapped and nailed to 2" × 4" studs, with 4" insulation batts. Exposed exterior wood has a penetrating preservative.

CLIENT: *Dr. and Mrs. Robert G. Stanley*
STRUCTURAL ENGINEER: *Haley W. Keister*
INTERIOR DESIGN: *Edward Heist, Jr.*

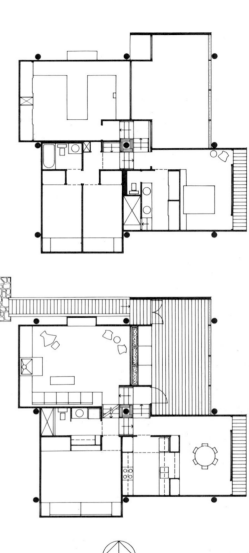

# AMELIA ISLAND DUNEHOUSES (project)

*Amelia Island, Florida, 1971*

Along with the Florida State Museum, this project marks the architect's unique explorations into the design of earth and architecture in unity—an avenue of design that has come to be called "earth architecture." But the Amelia Island Dunehouses project enters this special domain with special assertiveness, with a full and unequivocal statement.

## SITE

The design concept was derived, primarily, from the site, a coastal dune area approximately 1,800' wide measured between Florida A1A and the Atlantic Ocean shoreline. Within this width the houses would occupy a "band" approximately 600' wide. This band was about midway in the 1,800' coastal width. The natural vegetation—sand grasses, ground cover, and trees—would remain undisturbed.

There were to be two circulation systems, one for cars and one for pedestrians. The automobile system would be kept as minimal as possible by clustering parking in relation to the house groups. The pedestrian system would connect each house to a system of common paths, which would lead to the beach. Entrances to the individual house units were to face each other across a parking cluster area, a "trough" in form. The living room sides of the individual houses were also to face each other across a trough form, through which a pedestrian path would be woven. The vehicular and pedestrian zones would, thus, be completely separated.

With seventy-four units built as two- or three-bedroom structures in the third, or developed, zone, which was 10.6 acres, net density would be seven dwelling units per acre. This calculation does not include the beach, primary and secondary dune zone, or the forest zone along the road.

The houses were to be deployed in groups, the smallest group being pairs of houses, the largest containing six. The houses themselves were to be arranged in three irregular north-south rows. The outer rows were to have two-story units; the central row was to have three-story units. All houses were to be built into existing or augmented sand dunes.

In this site design we have a total of four distinct zones. Starting at the ocean, the first is the shoreline and beach zone, about 300' wide. It is left natural. The second zone contains primary and secondary dune formations,

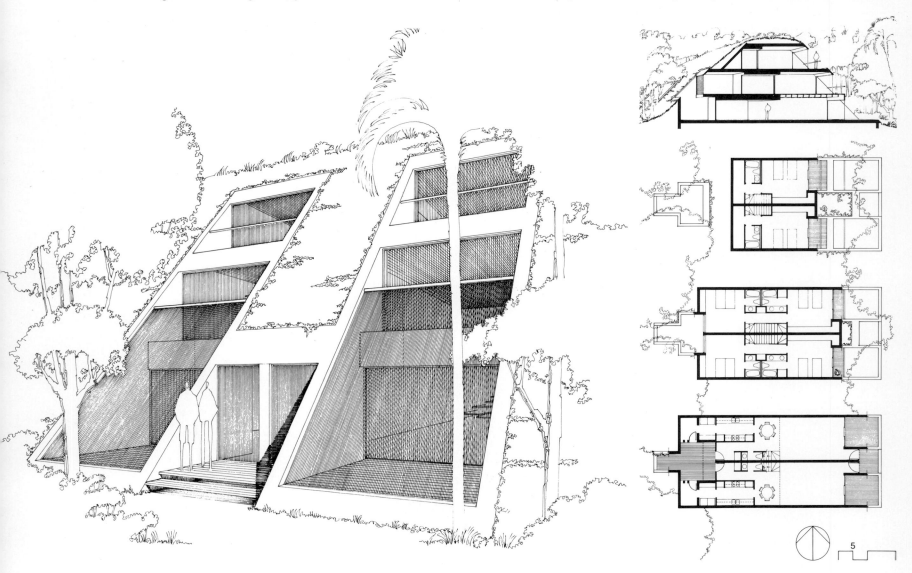

with vegetation firmly developed behind the secondary dune. This, too, is left natural, except for two carefully located footpaths threaded through the dunes. Like the beach, it is also about 300' wide. Third is the zone of houses, in the three irregular north-south rows, as just described. And fourth is still another preservation area, between the houses and the highway.

## STRUCTURE

The houses themselves were to be two or three stories high and would be built completely into the dunes, their entrances, windows, and balconies exposed on the dune slopes. The dunes are up to 35' high between trough and top. The two-story houses would be about 22' high to dune top, the three-story

35'. The angle of repose of the berms would be 1:1 or 1:2, depending on position. Sixteen inches of earth would cover the concrete slab structures. Lower floors were to be 4" above grade. Walls were to be built of reinforced concrete block braced with lateral concrete tie beams. Bottom-floor slab and roof slab were to be reinforced concrete. Intermediate floors were to be wood frame.

The three-bedroom units would contain 1,200 sf and have three baths. The two- and three-bedroom units would be identical in plan on their first and second floors, the two bedroom units being limited to two floors, without a third bedroom on a third floor. Overall, it could not have been a simpler idea. Nor could it have been more ingenious.

CLIENT: *Amelia Island Plantation*
STRUCTURAL ENGINEER: *Haley W. Keister*
MECHANICAL AND ELECTRICAL ENGINEER: *Roy Turknett Engineers*
CONTRACTOR: *Newman Construction Co.*

HWY A1A    NATURE PRESERVE    ROAD    PATHS    ROAD    PATHS    SECONDARY DUNE    PRIMARY DUNE    ATLANTIC OCEAN

50

# MORGAN RESIDENCE
*Atlantic Beach, Florida, 1971–1973*

William Morgan's house for his family of four (two sons) is very much along the lines of development of earth architecture. While not buried in the earth, its form is largely generated by the shape of the dune it inhabits, as well as by wind, light, and view. The house's shape is thus generated by family needs and natural forces, both resolved and expressed in architectural form.

It also increased public and professional knowledge of the architect, being his most publicized work to this point. The sectional drawing became one of his most reproduced illustrations, all but constituting an identifying logo.

A basic and strongly unifying geometry suggests, at first examination, a very simple spatial organization and floor plan. Further examination reveals that spatial organization and plan are a subtle if not ingenious resolution of complex family functions. But first, the geometry.

Three elements describe the form of the house. The first is the pyramidal or triangular massing, an extension in space of the form of the dune on which it sits. Second is the axial—almost ceremonial—plan composition, organized symmetrically on a central entrance and stair axis. Third is an ascending-descending progression of levels, six in all.

The entrance level is flanked by sheltered parking space for cars. This entrance places one on the central axis at the start. Entering the house, one descends two steps to the main living area. To the right is the dining room—kitchen area; to the left is the living room.

Both areas are equal in size. Ahead is a bisected but otherwise broad view of the ocean. This sense of spatial expanse has its counterpart in the lofting verticality of this common area's space, which is 20' deep, 30' wide, and nearly 30' to the ceiling peak, which is lit by a clerestory. A relatively small space proclaims a rather grand idea. The reason for this open family space was to assure that the family members—parents and two then about-to-be teenage sons—would share as much time as possible together. Their varied interests kept them apart most of the time.

Above this level are two more, the parents' area. It includes sleeping space, a study, baths, and storage. The baths and storage are slightly raised above the sleeping, constituting the uppermost level.

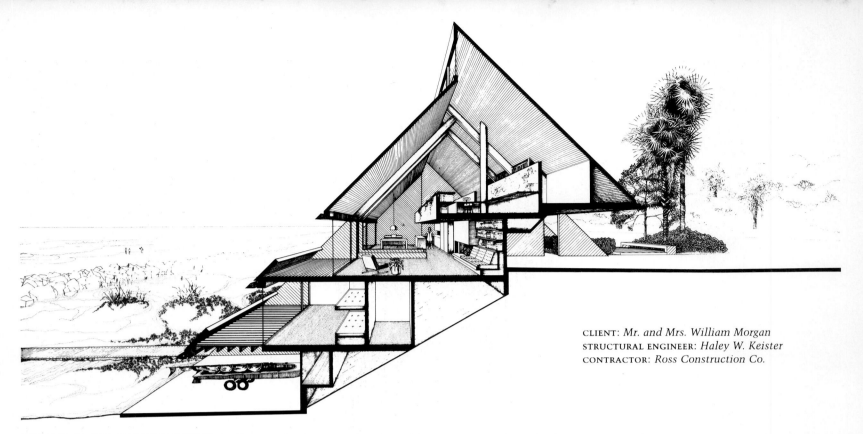

CLIENT: *Mr. and Mrs. William Morgan*
STRUCTURAL ENGINEER: *Haley W. Keister*
CONTRACTOR: *Ross Construction Co.*

Descending the stair from the family common space are two rooms with individual baths for the two sons. Both rooms have their own decks. Below this, at the bottom level, is an open sheltered area for beach equipment storage, boats, table tennis, and so on.

The central movement axis continues through a berm and a tree-sheltered sitting-picnic area and then to the beach beyond.

### SITE
The site is a narrow east-west rectangle, its east side fronting the beach—a site shape and orientation often found in Morgan's residential work. The site dimensions are 50' × 120', only one-seventh of an acre. The height of the dune on which the house sits was augmented slightly, using excavation material. Its height is about 17'.

### STRUCTURE
The house measures 30' to 35' × 68'5½" in plan form. It is 45' high measured from the beach side, almost 30' high from the street (entrance) side. It contains just under 1,800 sf of interior floor area.

There are four equal-size private decks totaling about 200 sf. The sheltered lower beach equipment storage area is about 599 sf, the two car ports under 600 sf.

The structure is wood frame on wood pilings with a concrete beam foundation. The main roof is supported by laminated wood beams, two of which are clearly presented in the living-dining space. Above-grade floors are wood frame. Exterior sheathing is bleached wood.

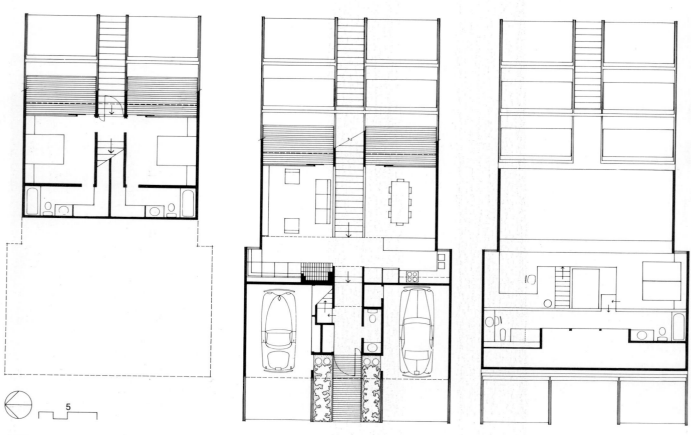

# ASSESSMENT

Lean years were to continue, 1967 being Morgan's most trying one: his total professional income was a meager $400. Service in the Naval Reserve, some lecturing, and the unfailing support of his wife, Bunny, saw him through. He entertained but resisted an offer to teach at Tulane University. But the tide turned in late 1968, with the commission to design the Jacksonville Children's Museum and, only two months later, another equally important project, the Florida State Museum in Gainesville.

The eight projects that illustrate this interval of Morgan's work are essays into two areas of architecture. One is the challenge of combining large units of repetitive form. The other is architecture's relationship to its earth site.

Interpod was an almost playful essay of combining architectural boxes, to see how many variations in applications could be achieved. The Goodloe residence can be seen as a direct application, with clear expression of the constituent units. The Ballentine residence utilizes a system of spatial boxes in such a way as to form an enveloping cube. The Stanley residence utilizes a system of spatial boxes in an ascending pinwheel, the entire configuration supported on nine wood posts.

The Jacksonville Children's Museum, now called the Museum of Arts and Sciences, employs architectural boxes in massive vertical disposition, one "box" at each of the building's corners. The four establish a spatial precinct, a transparent space several stories high. Here Morgan acknowledges the design for the National Center for Atmospheric Research in Colorado, designed by I. M. Pei (1964).

With the Florida State Museum, Morgan introduced the architectural theme with which his work has become largely identified—architecture in relation to earth form. Its concept has its sources in the Oakland Museum designed by Roche and Dinkeloo (1961) and the Etowah mound group in Cartersville, Georgia (A.D. 950–1550). The Florida State Museum is a series of earth-bermed levels, sheltering roofs, and ascending-descending terraces. As important, it is made of quite conventional building components, recalling the tenet of Morgan's deceased friend, Robert Ernest. That utilization of the everyday building system has remained a characteristic of Morgan's work.

The Amelia Island Dunehouses were an essay in designing an entire community in relation to a natural site, referring to and finding within the natural site's form the clues and themes for the entire design. This scheme was not to be realized, but Morgan adapted its premises to the design of his own home, a work that brought him considerable recognition.

Morgan's development of interest in architecture in relation to earth form has its roots in his own psyche, stirred as that was by his viewing of the great architecture of history, globally. It was sparked, at this stage of his career, by his meeting with the late Ripley Bullen, an archaeologist whom he met while working on the Florida State Museum in 1969. While in Bullen's office, Morgan happened to notice a plan on Bullen's desk. It was of an area only a few miles from where they were sitting. The site was Crystal River, an Indian earth-mound structure. So began a specific interest that was to culminate in Morgan's book *Prehistoric Architecture in the Eastern United States*, as well as further inform his design work.

1971–1973

# PYRAMID CONDOMINIUMS

*Ocean City, Maryland, 1971–1975*

The Pyramid Condominiums are located north of Ocean City, Maryland, which has become the principal resort city of the 200-mile-long Atlantic shore of the Delaware-Maryland-Virginia peninsula. Originally a town of summer cottages, it is now a year-round resort. Its development accelerated and soared in the late sixties and early seventies, and with that the decision was made to allow high-rise construction in a zone north of the town. The result has been a wall of high-rise structures. Among them Morgan's Pyramid Condominiums stands with special distinction.

Its form derives from an extension of the character of the beach landscape. The building's rise and fall are reminiscent of dunes and waves. The light-and-shade ripple appearance of its surface is a reminder of the wind-formed surface of a dune. The receding pyramid casts a smaller shadow on the beach than would a slab with the same ocean-view orientation. The building obeys a clear logic emanating directly from its own purpose: to provide many families with convenient seashore residences, with views of the ocean, easy access to the beach, a private outdoor area adjacent to their dwelling—and a distinct change of atmosphere.

The original design envisioned a staged development for an ultimate of 580 units. Only the first stage (shown here) of 171 units could be realized, largely due to the 1974 energy crisis and other factors.

The design is usefully examined from several points of view, starting with its purpose.

People come to the beach for a brief period—a weekend, a week, perhaps two weeks. A beach house should be easy to care for and can therefore be quite simple. Indeed, the simpler the better. It has to have places for gathering and for eating, and some private outside space. It has to be pleasant to be in when the weather is bad. It has to be easily heated, cooled, or ventilated. All this is fundamental, and is handily accomplished in this building.

A vacation place should also be a distinct change of environment, a special place. It is here that the Pyramid excels, for it is, as architecture, a place of happy and elegant occasion. It is a work of exuberant yet highly appropriate form. As such it is clearly superior to its neighbors.

The units are either one or two bedrooms,

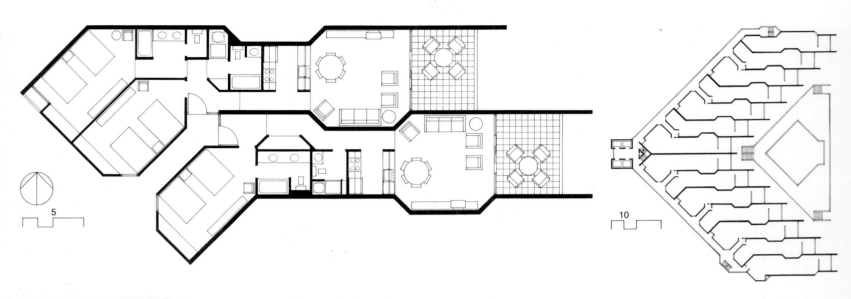

the bedrooms being on the inland side, living room—dining areas being on the ocean side, with balconies. Access to units is on the land side by means of an open corridor. The units are 11' wide at their narrow point (kitchen-bath corridor), 13½' wide at the entrance point, and either 11' (1 bedroom) or 22' (2 bedrooms) at the angled bedroom end. Living rooms are 16' wide. The private balconies are 10' × 13'. The plan is quite ingenious, the width variations achieved by a 45° stagger in plan layout. It is a plan well worth studying.

Vertically, the units are "pyramided" in sets of floors, with a side step-back every three floors. One out of three end units, at the step-backs, have extra large side terraces. The land-side access balcony terminates in stairs at both ends, the stairs serving for emergency egress and forming a sculptural termination to the horizontal lines of the balconies.

### SITE

The site for the first phase was a rectangular plot, 213' parallel to the beach and 515' deep, or 2½ acres. Of the 515' depth, the beach occupied over 100', the building itself a depth of 200', and the parking area another 200'. Parking was on one level, some under the building. The design allowed the later addition of a second parking level—a deck above the ground-level parking. This second level could also have tennis courts. The building occupies 16 percent of the site. The ground-level floor is open as a precaution to storm flooding. An elevated terrace on the beach side has a swimming pool.

The second phase was to have been built on an adjoining 5-acre site, with another 400' along the ocean as well as road frontage.

## BUILDING

The gross area of the building is 250,000 sf, of which 156,000 sf is in the form of one- or two-bedroom units. There are 78,000 sf of public access corridors and private terraces.

The structural bay spacing is 13'9". Floor-to-floor height is 8'6", floor-to-ceiling 8'. The building is nineteen stories high, plus penthouse and roof. Overall height is 220'. (Future phases were to have been thirteen stories and twenty-five stories, respectively.) The 45° geometry allowed 1.4 times more exposure on the inland side (bedrooms and entrances) than

on the ocean side (living rooms and private terraces).

The entire structure rests on deep pilings. Transfer beams carry the loads into vertical fin wells at the ground floor, thicker at the center of the building, thinner toward the sides. This is seen in the slab above the covered parking area. Reinforced concrete walls, 6" thick, support cast-in-place floor slabs. The walls resist lateral shear stress and reduce sound transmission.

The original idea of placing concrete walls was to utilize a spray-on concrete (not gunnite), which required light form work on one side only. This technique proved too slow. Uppermost bearing walls, where shear resistance permitted, were made of concrete blocks.

Construction of the transfer beams also proved costly.

A clear waterproofing was applied to the exterior concrete. Interior walls are conventional gypsum board on metal studs.

## MECHANICAL

A conventional mechanical system was used. Vertical riser shafts carry plumbing. The shafts terminate in a 20'-wide insulated collector chase in the first-floor ceiling, above sheltering parking. A central chiller is located on top of the elevator shaft. Air handling units have electric resistance strips in the ducts for heating.

CLIENT: *John S. Whaley*
STRUCTURAL ENGINEER: *Scherrer-Baumann and Associates*
MECHANICAL AND ELECTRICAL ENGINEER: *Atchison and Keller, Inc.*
INTERIOR DESIGN (MODEL): *John Saladino*
LIGHTING: *William Lam Associates*
CONTRACTOR: *The Farms Company*

# POLICE ADMINISTRATION BUILDING

*Jacksonville, Florida, 1971–1975*

As well as being an extremely interesting design statement in the development of William Morgan's design philosophy, this building is also a telling case study in the evolution of a building project.

The original intention was to build a building with two principal functions. One of these was to be public services, including five courtrooms, offices for public defenders, and related administrative offices. The other function was police operations headquarters. Parking for two hundred cars was to be provided on site. A program for a 200,000 gross sf facility was developed by Sidney Folse, a New Orleans architect and law enforcement specialist. The site was a two-block area in downtown Jacksonville, forming a 210' × 700' site, 3.4 acres. The site had a 15' slope.

It was also decided to hold a limited architectural design competition (open to architects in the northern Florida region). William Morgan won the competition, held in 1971. In awarding first prize, the jury commented that they had sought a design that was "airy rather than eerie." They also saw in this design an ease of approach and efficiency for handling everyday business.

The design was a system of low terracelike masses, with reposeful horizontal emphasis. The design was without windows, lighting coming from skylights. The courts and their related functions were located on the building's western end around an interior skylit atrium, accessible from a broad and welcoming system of terraced steps. The police operational and administrative functions were

located on the building's eastern end centered on a second atrium. The two atriums were connected by a skylit corridor passage. The design had four levels—a lower level for parking, services, and special police functions; a main level for the courts and additional police functions; a partial upper level, again for police functions; and a terraced roof level with gardens. The structural system utilized a 27' × 27' repetitive modular bay on the lower level, permitting 45° angled parking on the lower level, and a convenient office planning module above.

Shortly after the competition design was procured, a major change in the program occurred. The five courts and their related functions were deleted. The building was to be used for police operations only. The revision

of the design required considerable reconfigurations of interior space allocations, but it was possible to retain the original concept of the two atriums and their corridor passage link, all skylit. The west atrium with its grand stair entrance gave access to those functions that had a greater degree of need for public contact.

Design revision and development also allowed the refinement of the structural column system. It became a system of two-, three-, and four-story-high square-plan concrete "trees." The columns still were disposed on a 27' × 27' plan module. Their horizontal arms cantilevered 10'6" in two directions, leaving a 6' span to fill between "tree" perimeters.

The Italian architectural critic Fiamma Dinelli wrote that the building (referring to

the final design) achieved a brilliant resolution of three conflicting requirements, none being easily handled, even independently. First was a building requiring maximum security and with that highly controlled public accessibility. Second was a well-defined urban image—a sense of dignified public purpose. Third was a building that could be used freely by the public. The building had to be open and at the same time closed. It had to have a dignified appearance but not look overbearing.

The revised design solution accomplished the following:

1. All police services were consolidated under one roof.
2. Interdepartmental communication and interaction were encouraged.
3. A historic firehouse was preserved and incorporated into the design. (The competition design had also done this.)
4. A 2-acre rooftop garden was developed in an area otherwise lacking in such urban amenity. It is accessible from all four sides of the building.
5. Parking for 234 cars was provided.
6. The interior of the building was made cheerful by two linked atriums.
7. Interior circulation emphasized horizontal pedestrian movement rather than vertical elevator or escalator transport.
8. Interior halls were kept to a minimum.
9. Future expansion into the parking area was anticipated. A future parking structure north of the building will accommodate future needs.

## SITE

The site is in the center of Jacksonville, near other offices of local and state government. As mentioned, it covers an area of 3.4 acres and has an overall slope of 15'. Service access is at the east end. Automobile access is at three points, including a special entrance for auto servicing.

## STRUCTURE

The 27' × 27' concrete "trees," their perimeters 6' apart, compose the entire structure. The depth of the 27' × 27' horizontal concrete beam system is 3'. Thus, the 6' space between "tree" perimeters allows four 3' × 6' mechanical plenums. At the passage connecting the two atriums this 6' space becomes an elevated skylight. The edges of the concrete "tree" beams contain cove lighting.

The foundations are cast-in-place spread footings. The "tree" columns rest on these. Rooftop "trees" are located on the columns to avoid undue beam loading.

Exterior walls are rough-textured cast-in-place, fluted, and bush-hammered concrete with alternating bands of smooth-finished (rubbed) concrete. Roof terraces are broom-finished concrete and sodded earth.

Interior finishes include gypsum board walls, painted or vinyl covered. Ceilings are painted exposed concrete or hung metal slats under the beam-free 3' × 6' mechanical chases. Floors are glued-down nylon carpet. The final design had 207,667 gross sf of area, 147,444 net sf, for an efficiency of 71 percent; 234 parking spaces were provided.

## MECHANICAL

A roof-mounted cooling tower serves chillers at a lower level. Air is distributed by high-velocity ducts to variable air-volume units.

The building consumes 44,000 BTU / sf per year. The lighting load is 2 watts / sf per year. This is due to the windowless walls, the skylights, the planted roof garden, the small amount of glass, the air handling system, and the avoidance of elevator transport. It was able to meet 80 percent of the energy guidelines developed after its completion.

CLIENT: *City of Jacksonville*
STRUCTURAL ENGINEERS: *William J. Le Messurier (theory) and Haley W. Keister (project)*
MECHANICAL AND ELECTRICAL ENGINEER: *Roy Turknett Engineers*
LANDSCAPE ARCHITECT: *Diversified Environmental Planning*
INTERIOR DESIGN: *Edward Heist, Jr.*
LIGHTING: *William Lam Associates*
GRAPHIC DESIGN: *Meyer / Lomprey and Associates*
CONTRACTOR: *Orr Construction Co.*

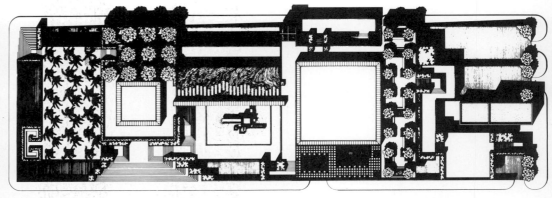

TERRACE LEVEL

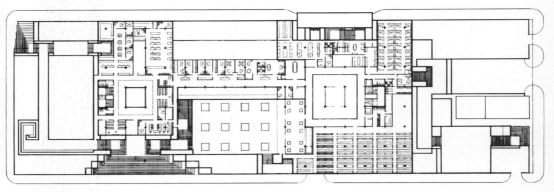

UPPER LEVEL

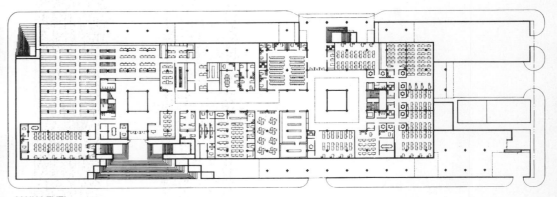

MAIN LEVEL

20

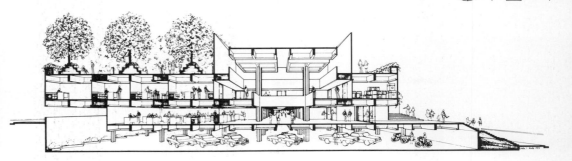

# MEMPHIS RIVERFRONT DEVELOPMENT (project)

*Memphis, Tennessee, 1972*

The 1950s ushered in a remarkable period of American planning, one that produced numerous highly imaginative and highly ambitious ideas for remaking cities. Special focus was placed on the city center and the waterfront. The plan for remaking downtown Memphis addressed precisely these elements.

The Washington, D.C.–based planning firm of Marcou, O'Leary developed the Memphis plan with consultants in the area of transportation, parking, and, not the least, urban design—that being William Morgan's contribution.

The center of the plan was the historic courthouse square, the core of Memphis' downtown. Adjacent to that is a civic center, a business district, and the riverfront. Nearby is a medical center. It was decided to remake

the riverfront into a combination of recreational park, housing, and automobile parking related to the downtown. The riverfront would also contain a railroad line and an automobile expressway. Immediately adjacent to the riverfront is the Wolf River. Mud Island formed a natural harbor area. Beyond it is the Mississippi River.

Morgan's design was a total concept for linking the city's core with the river and the island and, in so doing, provide the amenities and functions essential to revitalizing a twentieth-century city. The plan proposed 1,250 housing units, 2 hotels, multilevel parking for 4,000 cars, offices, shops, restaurants, and related activities. The shoreline areas and Mud Park (to be renamed Volunteer Bi-Centennial Park) would have 50 acres of park space, mari-

nas, a museum of the Mississippi, an outdoor theater, and a sports stadium.

Morgan's design proposal was a sculptural treatment of natural and urban landscape. The shoreline was to be sculpted into an angled slope for the Wolf River shores, the water there flowing more slowly than in the nearby Mississippi. A water-level fluctuation of 46' necessitated the sloped embankment.

From Court Square a spatial axis connected the city center to the rivers as an urban gateway. This axis would contain a blend of commercial space, hotels, restaurants, and terraced housing. The whole was composed as a receding series of terraces. Underneath would be automobile parking, an expressway, and a rail line. The terraced houses would have small private gardens along pedestrian promenades.

On the river side the houses would rise eight stories, a height of 80'. On the land side they would be four stories, a height of 50'.

The central connector axis was to angle northward to cross a bridge onto the island. There would be fine views of marina activity in the Wolf River basin and beyond to the Mississippi.

The project was to be built in five two-to-three-year phases, to be completed by 1988, a decade and a half. Its total cost was estimated to be approximately $150 million, of which a third would be public investment, two-thirds private. This was for the entire core program, the waterfront being a portion of it.

In retrospect such projects may, at first viewing, seem to be somewhat conjectural, possibly utopian. This one, in fact, seems more and more reasonable as one examines it. It could have been done. It certainly is needed. In prospect, it is very much a model of the level of imagination our cities need.

CLIENT: *Memphis Downtown Planning Program*
PLANNING CONSULTANT: *Marcou, O'Leary, and Associates*
TRANSPORTATION PLANNING: *Alan M. Voorhees and Associates*
PARKING PLANNING: *William S. Pollard Consultants*

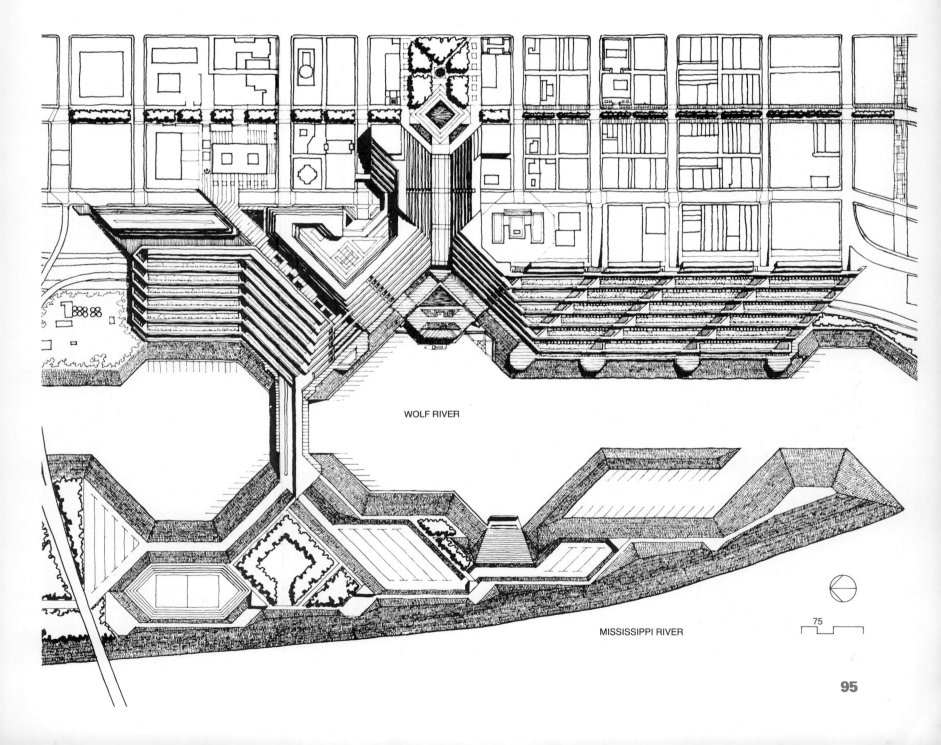

WOLF RIVER

MISSISSIPPI RIVER

75

# MORGAN OFFICE BUILDING

*Jacksonville, Florida, 1972–1973*

Originally housing a livery stable and blacksmith shop, this two-story brick structure was built shortly after Jacksonville's great fire in 1901. The ground floor came to be used as a parking garage, the upper floor a printing loft. Columns and beams were strengthened to carry the weight of the presses. Well before the federal tax incentive for preserving old buildings was enacted, Morgan acquired the structure and rehabilitated it.

The ground floor has an office suite, parking for nineteen cars, and an entrance lobby for the upper floor. That, in turn, has six office suites for law firms as well as Morgan's two-level office.

Morgan was particularly conscientious in respecting the original character of the structure on its exterior, while making full use of its interior composition—robust columns, sturdy brick bearing walls, and exposed wood floor and ceiling framing. In his own office he purposefully avoided having new interior partitions interrupt the continuity of the unadorned brick bearing wall. He went so far as to replant street trees along the sidewalk in their original locations.

## SITE
The site measures 82′ × 105′, including a 7′-wide side alley. Site area is one-fifth of an acre.

## STRUCTURE
The structure is brick exterior bearing wall, with a post-and-beam interior system on an 18′ × 20′ module. The first floor has a height of 14′; the second, 16′8″, which made an upper level, or mezzanine, possible in Morgan's office area. The building has a gross area of 12,800 sf. Upper-floor lighting is supplemented with north-facing monitors.

CLIENT: *Morgan Properties*
STRUCTURAL ENGINEER: *Haley W. Keister*
MECHANICAL AND ELECTRICAL ENGINEER: *Roy Turknett Engineers*
CONTRACTOR: *Newman Construction Co.*

WILLIAM MORGAN ARCHITECTS

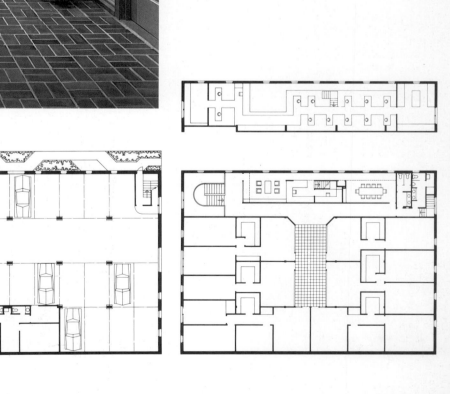

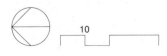

10

# INTERAMA AMPHITHEATER (project)

*1974*

The purpose of this structure was to foster international trade and cultural exchange. The program specified a 6,000-person amphitheater, a 10,000-sf exhibition center, and a 400-seat restaurant. A floating stage would permit stage performances or, when removed, water pageants. The exhibit hall would be located beneath the seating, the restaurant beneath one of two ascending entrance ramps.

Hovering above the seating would be a tensile roof, supported on six masts and guyed with cables. The roof would have been covered with Teflon-coated fiberglass. Had it been built, it would have been the largest tensile roof then in existence. It was the concept of the engineer Horst Berger, based on the work of Frei Otto. The roof would have to have been capable of withstanding hurricane winds. Its purpose would be to create a sense of place commensurate with the function of the project and to provide shelter against sun and rain.

## SITE
The site was a shorefront area on Biscayne Bay. A 30'-high artificial hill was to have been formed. The public entrance would be from a central point on the west. From there two entrance ramps would direct the audience northward and southward to the seating area. The southward ramp would coil over the restaurant area before passing as a bridge into the seating area. Truck service for the underseating exhibit area was to be at the north.

## STRUCTURE
Engineer Horst Berger explained the principle of tensile structures in an article in *Architectural Record* (February 1975). The advantages are relative ease of assembly (with a skilled construction crew), a minimum of material, great wind and storm load resistance, a high degree of flexibility in form, rapid construction, easy repair, and esthetic power.

Like a warped spiderweb or stretched net, structural stability depends on all members being in tension and disposed in three dimensions. This prevents any lateral movement from occurring. A consequence of these conditions is that the cable members pull each other in opposite directions. This, in turn, requires a disposition of cables as curves or arcs, which, pulling in opposite directions, form opposing curves. Such a form is called "anticlastic" or "opposing curvature." A potato chip and a saddle are commonplace examples of anticlastic forms. (A synclastic form has one or more surfaces that curve in the same direction, examples being a dome or a barrel.)

The thin shell-concrete roof textures designed by the Mexican Félix Cándela are anticlastic structures of concrete, the forces acting in compression. The tensile roof is an anticlastic structure acting in tension. It offers greater flexibility in form, it is easier to erect over very large open areas, and its individual components can be varied.

The free-form seating design has its roots in that of Greek and Roman theaters, the naturalistic shape recalling an unrealized project of Alvar Aalto to utilize an ancient fortification in Siena, Italy, as an outdoor amphitheater.

CLIENT: *Inter American Center Authority, State of Florida*
TENSILE STRUCTURAL ENGINEER: *Horst Berger, Geiger-Berger Associates*
CIVIL, FOUNDATION, ELECTRICAL, AND MECHANICAL ENGINEER: *H. J. Ross Associates*
ACOUSTICS: *Christopher Jaffe*
THEATER DESIGN: *Jules Fischer*

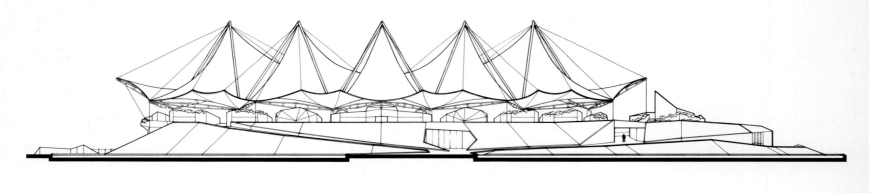

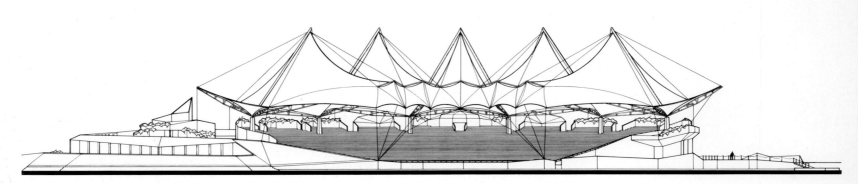

# NORFOLK TOWNPOINT (project)

*Norfolk, Virginia, 1973–1975*

Morgan's project for redeveloping a large portion of the waterfront area of Norfolk recalls his design for the Pyramid Condominiums in Maryland as well as the design for the Memphis redevelopment. The redevelopment shown consists of 1,600 dwelling units. In a larger sense, this project characterizes some of the more ambitious "megastructure" thinking of the sixties and seventies.

In this design—and characteristic of those megastructure essays—an individual cellular entity is multiplied repetitively to form an immense whole. The cell itself is capable of being combined with considerable formalistic flexibility. It can be disposed in straight lines or at a 45° angle. Through the vertical stacking of cells, height can be stepped up or down or kept uniform. (Morgan's design is, for the most part, uniform in height.)

All this combines to offer an industrialized system for remaking a large urban area. It allows a high degree of construction systematization and organization. It allows an intricate "fit" between old urban fabric and new. It makes possible a marriage between individual privacy and an overall community of activities and interests.

This type of design, seldom realized but often posed, begs the question of the use of industrial methods in addressing the urban problems of great importance in our time. We have in this a challenge to use our technology at its best—material, organizational, and fiscal. In this we see not so much an architectural utopia as much as a persistent question.

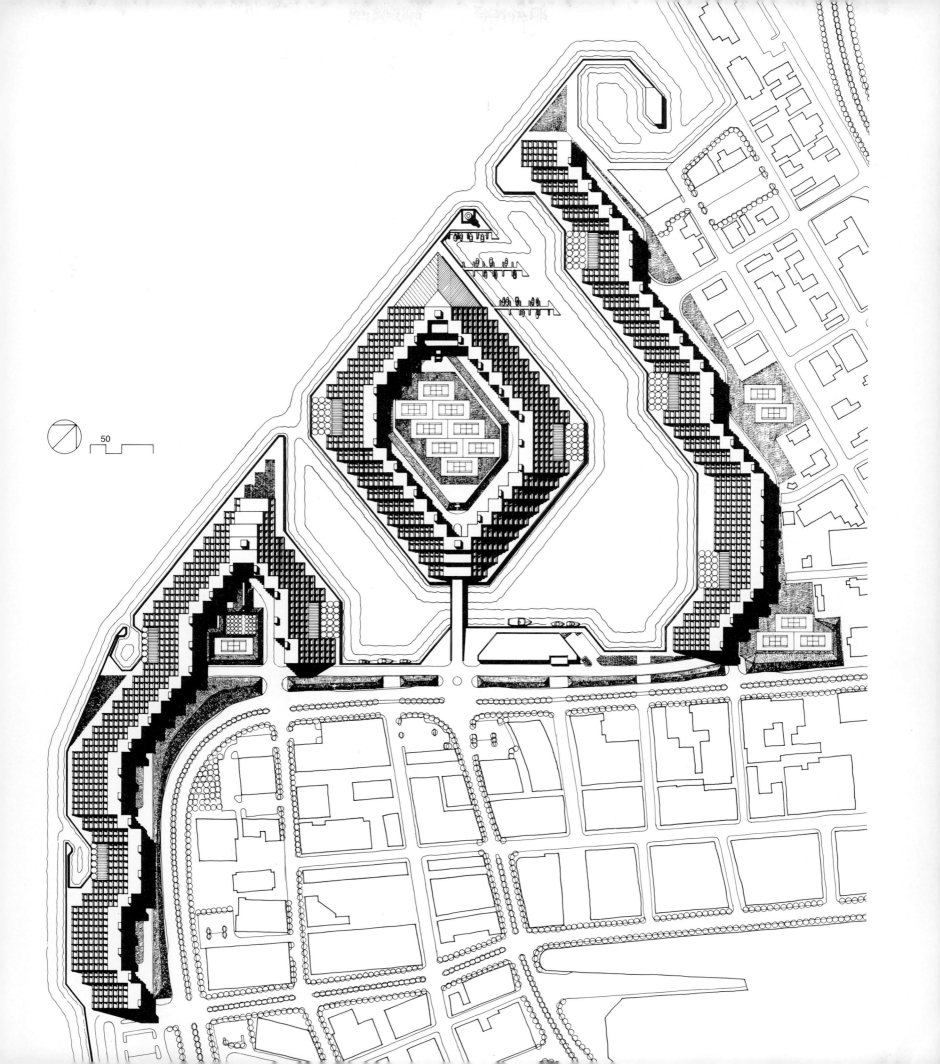

# ASSESSMENT

A highlight of this period in Morgan's practice was winning first prize in the design competition for the Jacksonville Police Administration Building. In 1970 his office was relocated from Atlantic Beach to rented space in the former ballroom atop a high-rise building in Jacksonville. In 1972 a former livery stable became available. It was acquired by Morgan and remodeled as his own office, with additional rented suites. With the commission for the Police Administration Building and the relocation of the office, Morgan's practice had come to know stability. The buildings of this interval are both extensions and enlargements of his previous inclinations and pursuits.

The Pyramid Condominiums in Ocean City, Maryland, combine spatial box "elements" into a whole, the form articulated by the boxes and constituting an expressive mass in itself. In this building we have the ingenuity of arrangement found in the earlier houses composed of spatial box elements. They play a key visual role in the appearance of the overall building mass.

The Police Administration Building, whose plan may be compared to that of Fatehpur Sikri in India (1569–1574), is again a composition of square modules. The particular innovation of this building is the utilization of a 27' × 27' square concrete "tree" structure. Fatehpur Sikri is a system of modular cells and courtyards; this building is a system of uniform cellular elements with two connected internal spaces.

The "tree" itself has several attributes. It establishes the planning module; it is the structural system; it is capable of being used at different heights; and it can be "stacked" vertically, "tree" upon "tree." Between the "trees," at their crown, a resulting two-directional ceiling space becomes a plenum for mechanical components—ducts, electric cables, and so on. The particular advantage of this system is that it is capable of needed variations, and, at the same time, its function is given clear visual expression. Many module systems as well as structural systems are quite invisible. Here one has an integrated system that is visually expressed.

The Memphis Riverfront Development project together with the Norfolk Townpoint project, done two years later, were essays in applying modular repetitiveness to the existing form of a site, as well as its urban texture. Both were "city edge" configurations, both for high density. Both draw a degree of inspiration from the plan of the Funerary Temple of Queen Hatshepsut in Egypt (1500 B.C.), the Lake George mound group in Holly Bluff, Mississippi (A.D. 800–1500), and Prah Vihear, Cambodia (A.D. 1050–1150). All are vast and ordered configurations on the landscape.

The Morgan offices (formerly a livery stable below a printing company) provided an early exercise in historic restoration and modified use.

The Interama Amphitheater project draws on Morgan's own earlier work while in Italy as well as the structural system of a cable-supported roof membrane, developed by the German engineer Frei Otto and compellingly demonstrated at the Montreal Expo 67. Its seating arrangement may be studied in relation to those of ancient Greek amphitheaters as well as the recent projects of the Finnish architect Alvar Aalto.

Surely a capstone to this interval of work is the Hilltop House. It is Palladian in its purity of compositional concept, but the universality of this idea goes well beyond. One can compare it to the Villa Rotunda by Palladio and Boroburdur, Java (A.D. 800–850). William Morgan's design palette was enlarging, firmly.

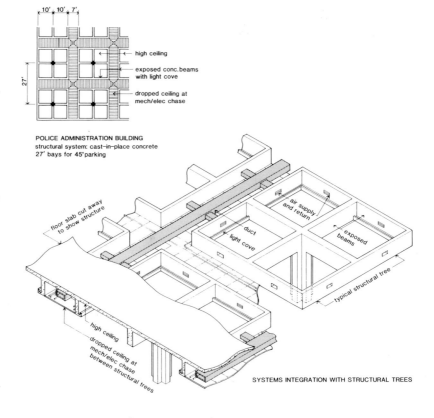

high ceiling
exposed conc. beams with light cove
dropped ceiling at mech/elec chase

POLICE ADMINISTRATION BUILDING
structural system: cast-in-place concrete
27' bays for 45' parking

floor slab cut away to show structure
air supply and return
duct
light cove
exposed beams
typical structural tree
high ceiling
dropped ceiling at mech/elec chase between structural trees

SYSTEMS INTEGRATION WITH STRUCTURAL TREES

1973–1976

# DICKINSON RESIDENCE

*Atlantic Beach, Florida, 1973*

This beach house faces eastward to the Atlantic Ocean. The site is subject to sudden and violent storms. The stepped berm protects against them and at the same time serves as a sunbathing area, the steps and terraces lessening the need for outdoor furniture, which is subject to severe weathering in this climate. Beach furniture must also be able to be removed quickly.

The steps and terraces are infilled with Mexican tile. Aside from their functional purpose, they form a visually dynamic base for the visually passive mass of the house.

The house is a simple rectangular box in two stories. On the lower floor are common family spaces; the upper floor, bedrooms.

The general composition—berm-and-rectangular structure—is a classical if not universal theme in architectural composition. The historical reference, in this case, was the Palace of the Governors in Uxmal, Mexico.

CLIENT: *Mr. and Mrs. Maxwell K. Dickinson*
STRUCTURAL ENGINEER: *H. W. Keister Associates*
CONTRACTOR: *Ross Construction Co.*

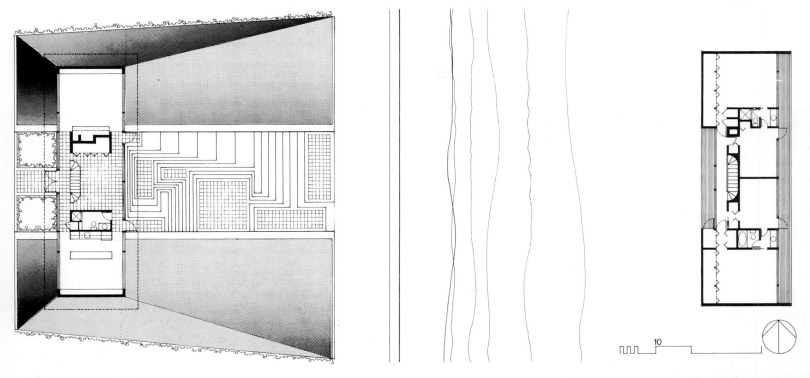

# ATLANTIC BEACH DUNEHOUSES

*Atlantic Beach, Florida, 1974–1975*

Few of William Morgan's projects attracted as much attention from the design profession as well as the public as did the two side-by-side "dunehouses." They were built at a time of special concern for environmental protection and energy conservation. They are, as much as anything else, highly elegant architectural designs.

Located alongside Morgan's own residence, the dunehouses occupy a modest lot bordering the coast. A coastal road provides access and parking on the west. The houses look eastward toward the ocean.

The plan form of the two houses resembles two adjoining eggs. Each measures 17'6" in width by 38'6" in length.

The site measures 50' × 175', the two houses 35' × 35'. The houses protrude 6' above grade on the entrance side and 17' above the beach level. Each house has two floor levels. The houses are entered by descending a common stair. The upper floor of each house has an entrance, bath, and sleeping area, which also overlooks a lower living area. Reached by a flowing stair, the lower floor has a living area, kitchen with dining area, storage area, and utility area. Each unit has 750 sf of floor area.

Being as wide as it is high, this small amount of floor area has a generously spatial character. The window-door, opening eastward onto a terrace, allows ample interior daylight.

The entire structure was built of concrete. The lower portion is conventional cast-in-place concrete. On that an egg-shaped system of steel reinforcing rods was set, forming continuous walls and roof. Wire mesh was fastened to the reinforcing to serve as a base for a "gunite," or spray-on, concrete shell. The concrete was placed in two operations to a thickness of between 2½" and 4". After curing, the shell was covered with 20" of earth. The lower cast-in-place portion of the structure is similar to that of a swimming pool. The upper, sprayed-on portion can be likened to a submarine.

The steel reinforcing is not needed for structural strength since the concrete is in compression. Of course, it does stabilize the concrete, acting as temperature reinforcing. Its primary function was to establish the shell's form. That was calculated by computer, which established a system of dimension coordinates.

A heat pump provides interior heating and cooling. Interior temperature is easily maintained at 70°F, largely due to the insulation of the shell's earth cover. Early-morning sun shining into the east opening required a shielding blind. Humidity did not prove to be a problem. Sound is easily absorbed by interior finishes—wood and fabrics.

The carpet is sand color so as to lessen the obvious problem of foot-borne sand from the beach. The contrast between structure and outfitting is clearly stated in the visual interplay between concrete (support) and the interior's wood and fabric (furnishings, finishes). The concealed lighting between stair and wall further articulates roles.

The architect likens the concept of the interior, particularly the proportions of the interior spatial volume and the flowing stair, to the grand entrance of the Laurentian Library in Florence, Italy, designed by Michelangelo. It is a fitting comparison, a great spatial moment having been created in a modest volume.

The dunehouses illustrate Morgan's use of the proportions of squares and golden rectangles. Their numerical ratios are 1 : 1 and 1 : 1.6180339 . . . , respectively. The golden section appears in the proportions of the Parthenon on the Acropolis of Athens, in the work of Le Corbusier, and in many other examples of Western architecture. It also appears in the spiral form in pine cones, the heads of normal daisies, certain sea shells, and the horns of some animals. Elsewhere in nature the golden section is found in the shapes of flowers, ferns, butterflies, water currents, and many other places.

The proportion may be derived mathematically by the following formula, in which the number, $n$, represents the value of the golden section:

$$n = .5 + \sqrt{(.5)^2 + 1}.$$

Thus, the golden proportion has the value of 1.6180339. . . . An unusual mathematical characteristic of the number is that, multiplied times itself, it equals itself plus one:

$$n^2 = n + 1 \text{ or } 2.618 = 1.618 + 1.$$

The mathematical value of the golden section is the only number that equals one when one is subtracted from it and the balance is multiplied by the number itself:

$$(n - 1)n = 1 \text{ or } (.618)1.618 = 1.$$

The value of the golden proportion in architecture stems, in part, from its clarity. The golden rectangle cannot be mistaken for a square. One of its sides is distinctly longer than the other. A geometric property of the golden proportion is that a square added to its long side produces a larger golden rectangle.

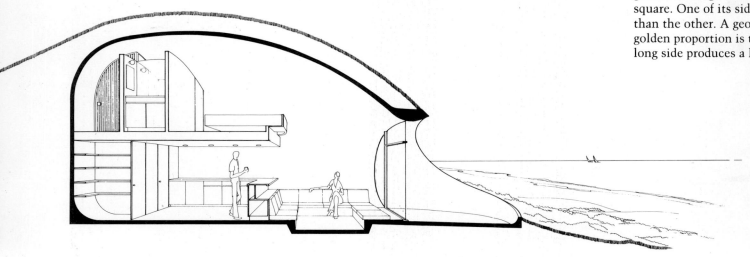

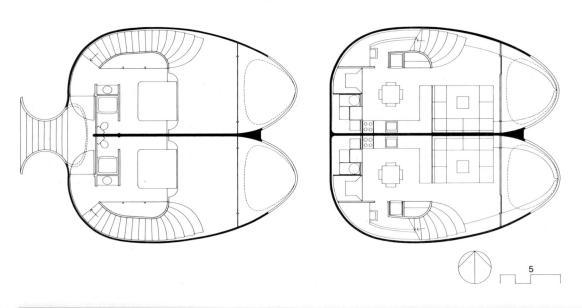

Similarly, a square subtracted from the short side of a golden rectangle yields a smaller golden rectangle.

The dimensions of the Atlantic Beach Dunehouses utilize the golden proportion extensively. Both the curved surfaces and the flat planes of the two units are regulated by it. The party wall separating the units is equidistant from the north and south exterior walls (1 : 1). Both units are 17.5' wide. The length of both units is approximately 28.3', measured from the exterior wall to the west to the sliding glass doors facing east. Thus, the length-to-width ratio of the lower-level plan is 28.3 : 17.5, very nearly 1.618 : 1. The upper-level plan of each level is based on a 17.5' square. The width of the porch at the east end of each unit is 10.8', the difference between the lengths of the upper- and lower-level plans (1.618−1).

The upper-level plan is further subdivided by the regulating lines of smaller squares and golden rectangles. The width of the entry porch approximates the width of the interior stair (1 : 1). The ratio of the width to length of the bathroom is about 1 : 1.618. The width of the vanity very nearly equals the distance from the mirror wall above the lavatory to the plane of the closet doors (1 : 1), and so on. The same proportions regulate both the sections and the elevations of the dunehouses.

STRUCTURAL ENGINEER: *Geiger-Berger Associates*
MECHANICAL AND ELECTRICAL ENGINEER: *Roy Turknett Engineers*
LIGHTING: *William Lam Associates*

# PERDUE OFFICE BUILDING (project)

*Salisbury, Maryland, 1974*

The landscape of the "Delmarva" peninsula (Delaware-Maryland-Virginia) is one of horizontal emphasis, the sky filling much of the scenery. It is reminiscent of the American plains. Its main activity is agriculture, including raising chickens for the East Coast market.

Perdue, Inc., purchases, processes, and markets Delmarva chickens. It has risen to a position of prominence in volume and quality. William Morgan's design was to house the headquarters operations of the Perdue company. The building was to be, essentially, a computer-centered administrative office. The design would have both blended with and complemented the landscape.

The 65-acre site was wooded, with low hills. Morgan designed a structure 156' × 156', about 400' from a highway. The site plan was organized so that a parking area did not obscure the view of the building from the approach road.

The structure itself was to be set between two low hills, its roof forming a horizontal line between the hill tops. A stone cube and a broad fascia above the building's entrance would have constituted a subtle signal of the building's presence in the otherwise uninterrupted landscape. Indeed, the design would have increased rather than diminished the landscape's intrinsic personality.

The building interior was to be a square, its center a raised operations area above a computer center. The raised area would have had open views to surrounding office areas. Lighting was to be through a rooftop skylight, which would admit a reflected light, and four lateral openings. Of these two would have had views of side courts, one a view of a proposed artificial lake, which would have been formed by excavation used to amplify the slopes flanking the building's sides. The whole area was to be reforested.

The original building was to have 25,000 sf of floor area. An additional 28,000 sf for expansion could have been added on the sides.

The view from the main highway to the north would have been across the lake. Altogether it would have been a model of elegance and regionally sensitive design.

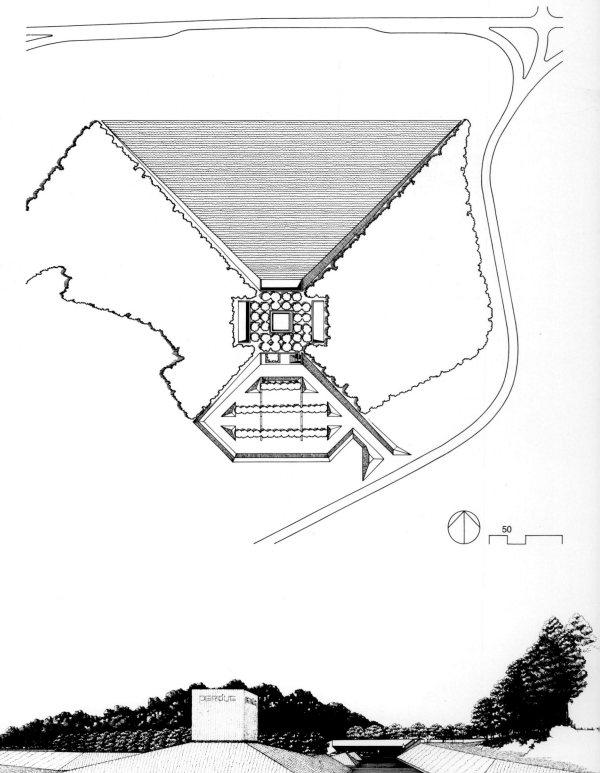

CLIENT: *Perdue, Inc.*

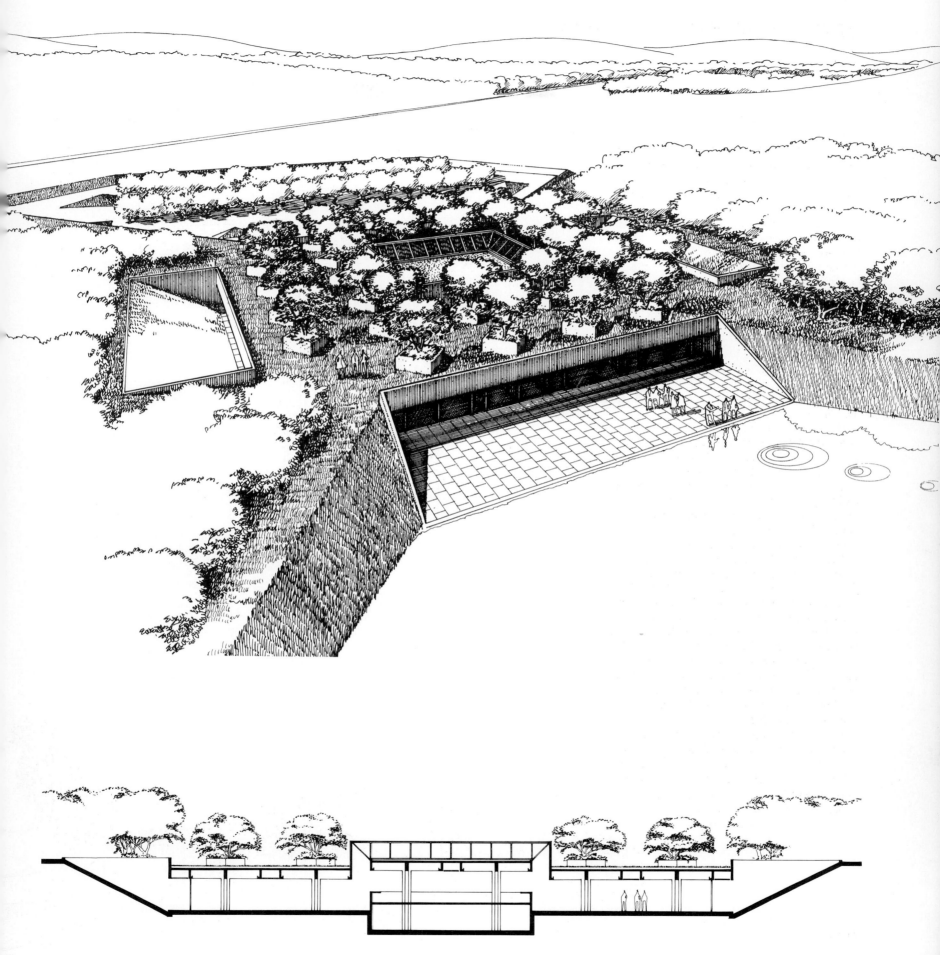

# BEACH HOUSE
*Ponte Vedra Beach, Florida, 1974–1976*

This beach house may be usefully examined as a further exploration of the concept of the Hilltop House, which preceded it by a few years.

Again, the site has a west-to-east orientation, with a view to the Atlantic Ocean. The site measures 100' × 336'. On it the house form is disposed as a square berm, measuring 99' × 99'. Within that the house sits, also square in plan form and measuring 60' × 60'. It is composed of 12' × 12' plan modules.

The client sought a house with an ocean view for all major rooms, through ventilation, spatial continuity in the interior, large automobile garages, an insect-screened enclosure large enough for a swimming pool, beach access to showers, and accommodations for four children. Privacy to the north and south was

also required, as those neighboring sites were expected to be developed.

The design is a visually passive low pyramid rising two stories. An enclosed swimming pool and garden face the ocean. Earth berms flank the sides and form an entry court. A two-story-high living-dining area opens diagonally toward the sea.

All bedrooms have diagonally disposed views of the ocean. Two are on the lower floor, two on the upper. The ceilings of the lower-floor bedrooms rise to the sloped sides of the pyramid roof. They also receive side light from court recesses in the berm.

The entrance is an elegant forecourt. The plan is one of the architect's best resolved, meriting careful study.

The house is built on a concrete slab. Its

structure is concrete block and wood frame. The exterior is stucco, the roof wood shingles. The house comprises 2,800 sf of air-conditioned space.

CLIENT: *Mr. and Mrs. Hayne D. McCondichie*
STRUCTURAL ENGINEER: *H. W. Keister Associates*
MECHANICAL AND ELECTRICAL ENGINEER:
*Roy Turknett Engineers*
LANDSCAPE ARCHITECT: *Wayne O. Manning*
CONTRACTOR: *Dave Plummer Construction Co.*

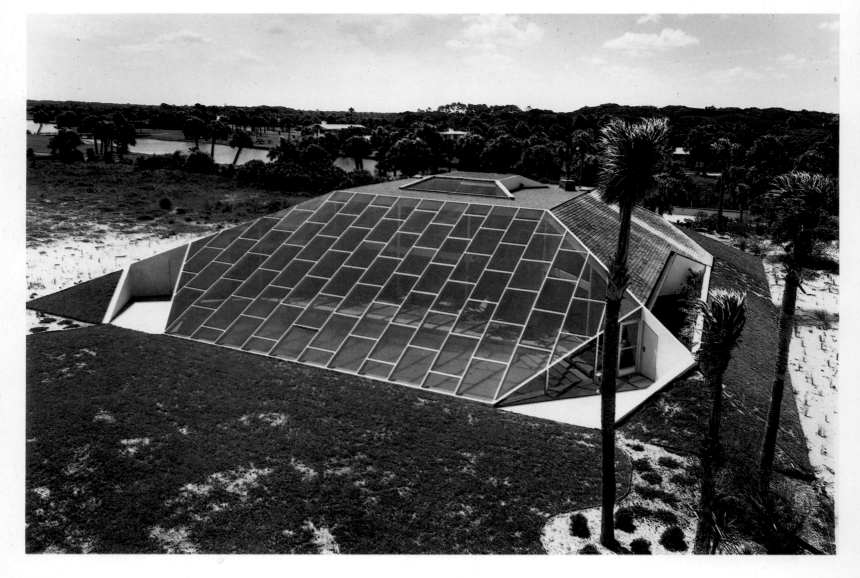

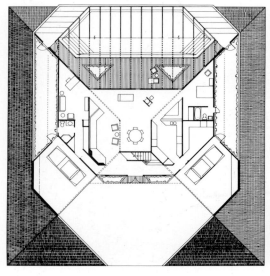

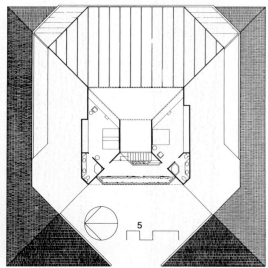

# DANIEL BUILDING

*Jacksonville, Florida, 1975–1979*

Originally known as the State of Florida Regional Service Center, this building serves the needs of several state agencies in the region.

Its primary attraction is its architectural form—a series of stepped terrace floors creating a partial pyramid form. This configuration has become a particularly compelling notion in modern architecture but an equally difficult one to handle.

The building has three principal elements. First is its main function, a state office building containing approximately 200,000 sf of office space and housing some 900 workers. Second is its function as a parking garage for 600 cars. Third is its public function as a riverfront promenade, viewing place, and outdoor theater.

The office building is arranged on five floor levels, each equal in length but varying in depth. They adjoin and cover the ramped three-level parking structure to the rear. The promenade and terraces are extensions of the office floors toward the St. Johns River, which is viewed to the south. A portion of the parking garage has a flat floor, which could be readily converted to office space. It is also conceivable that the remaining garage areas could be converted to office use. This would be possible in the future should access by public transit be more fully developed. Alteration of the ramps would also be needed.

Interior circulation is by means of a centrally located three-cab passenger elevator bank and a central interior stair. A freight elevator and fire stairs are located at the build-ing's ends. The central interior stair, lit by indirect natural light, creates a strong visual connection between floors.

As originally conceived, all five of the office floors would have had open southward views to the river. The top three floors, in addition, have northward views. The south side of the top-floor offices have an access corridor. Unfortunately, due to fire code requirements, the south views from the top-floor offices are blocked, the corridor partition being a windowless solid wall rather than being glazed. Such details are extremely important, but are largely matters of office operation policies, somewhat beyond the control of the architect. In any case, the problem of the blocked vista is amenable to correction.

## SITE
The site measures 365′ × 380′, forming an area of just over 3 acres. The building itself occupies 66 percent of the site, its dimensions being 301′ × 306′. A portion of the building occupies the air rights of a federal highway at the northwest corner. The garage is city owned. The state office building is built in the air rights above the city garage.

## STRUCTURE
The entire building is laid out on a 5′ × 5′ module, a convenient office dimension. The structural module is 25′ × 60′, derived from the required dimensions for automobile parking. Both columns and beams are double, creating a space at the center of all pairs. This space is used as a mechanical chase for ducts and conduits. The space is 2′8″ wide. Floor thickness is 3′9″ deep, including beams. The overall effect is to reduce overall building volume.

The lighting, acoustic treatment, air handling ducts, and electric conduit are integrated into this structural system. Fluorescent lights illuminate an acoustic ceiling board to provide diffused indirect ceiling light. This is increased by desk-level task lighting. The fluorescent lights are in three lengths and can be easily changed.

The height from the floor to the bottom of the beam is 8′. Movable partitions fit into tracks. Where partitions do not coincide with beams, a glass filler panel is used. Interior floor-to-ceiling heights are 8′ and 10′. Cantilevers are 15′.

The terrace canopy consists of two cable-supported inverted cones held by two masts. The canopy measures 45′ × 105′.

The varying floor plan depths facilitate accommodation of agency offices of different sizes. The building's silhouette reduces the obstruction of the river view from other buildings. The full vertical dimension of the building is expressed in the interior at the elevator lobby.

## MECHANICAL
State law required a life-cycle energy cost analysis. A 100 percent variable air volume cooling and constant perimeter electric heat system was used. Studies were made between systems using air-cooled and water-cooled chillers, with and without economizer cycle. A water-cooled chiller without economizer cycle was chosen. Analysis projected an energy consumption of 51,000 BTU / sf / year, or 7 percent below the U.S. GSA standard of that time. The state standard was then 66,000 but was subsequently lowered to 46,800.

## MATERIALS
The building is built of precast prestressed structural beams. Columns and floor slabs are poured in place. Cantilevered concrete sun shades shield the insulated double glazing. The concrete is exposed. Structural elements are smooth finished; nonstructural concrete surfaces are fluted and bush hammered.

## COST
The cost of the building was $8,918,000 or $36 / sf. Car parking was $2,850 / space.

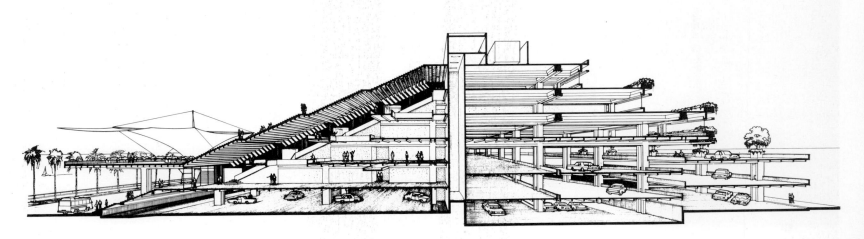

138

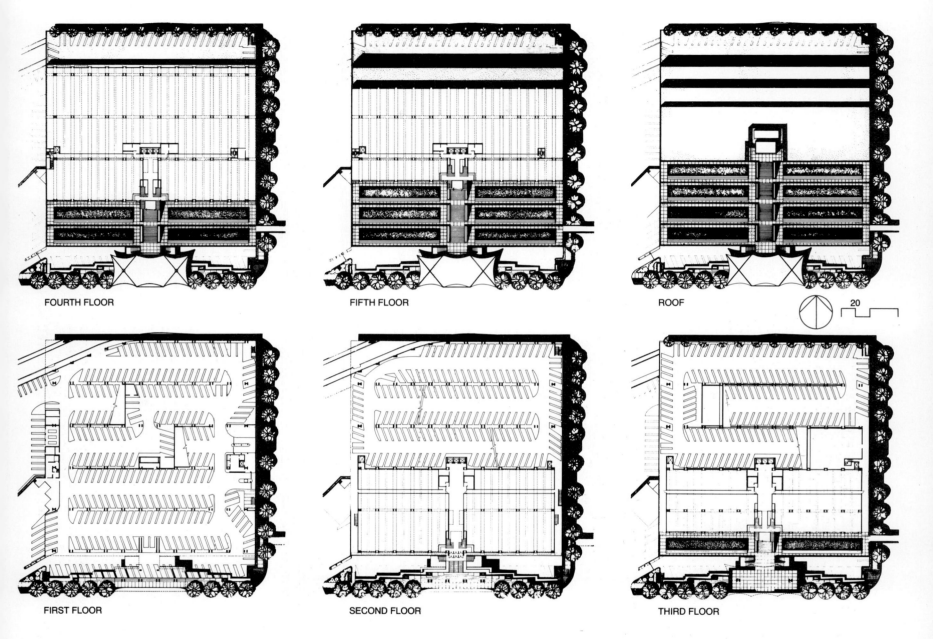

FOURTH FLOOR

FIFTH FLOOR

ROOF

20

FIRST FLOOR

SECOND FLOOR

THIRD FLOOR

CLIENT: *Department of General Services, State of Florida*

STRUCTURAL ENGINEER: *H. W. Keister Associates*

MECHANICAL AND ELECTRICAL ENGINEER: *Roy Turknett Engineers*

LANDSCAPE ARCHITECT: *Diversified Environmental Planning*

INTERIOR DESIGN: *Vida Stirbys Brown*

PARKING CONSULTANT: *Conrad Associates*

CONCRETE CONSULTANT: *Concrete Consulting Corp.*

CANOPY CONSULTANT (STRUCTURAL): *Geiger-Berger Associates*

CANOPY CONSULTANT (ACOUSTIC): *Christopher Jaffe*

CONTRACTOR: *Reinhold Construction Co.*

**139**

# CHARLESTON MUSEUM (project)

*Charleston, South Carolina, 1975*

This design was a submission in an open competition. The design concept derives from an attempt to integrate a new building form into the texture of a historic city. Though much larger, the design would defer to the historic Joseph Manigault House to the south of the site. The proposed museum site was the paddock area of the Manigault House.

This design proposed a one-story structure, its floor level 6′ below street level to maintain an overall low mass. A corner entrance would give access to visitor facilities, including orientation, as well as the museum's administrative offices. From there, and grouped around an interior court, regularly proportioned exhibit galleries could be reached. The court could also serve for exhibits. A service entrance and staff parking would be located opposite the visitor entrance side. In addition, the roof was to be treated as a public garden, with views inward to the court, outward to the surrounding city.

A 20′ × 80′ structural bay was proposed, again using the paired column-and-beam configuration. Integrating lighting, air handling, sound control, and electric conduits, this system would facilitate exhibit design and gallery flexibility. The exterior character of the building would harmonize with the Charleston setting. Red brick was proposed to fill the spaces between concrete structure. All masonry would be offset by ample greenery.

The building would have had an area of 94,600 sf above grade on a 136,332 sf site. Thus, the building would cover 87 percent of the site.

The design may be compared with the Museum of History and Anthropology in Mexico City, designed by Pedro Ramírez Vasques, as well as the Oakland Museum, designed by Roche and Dinkeloo.

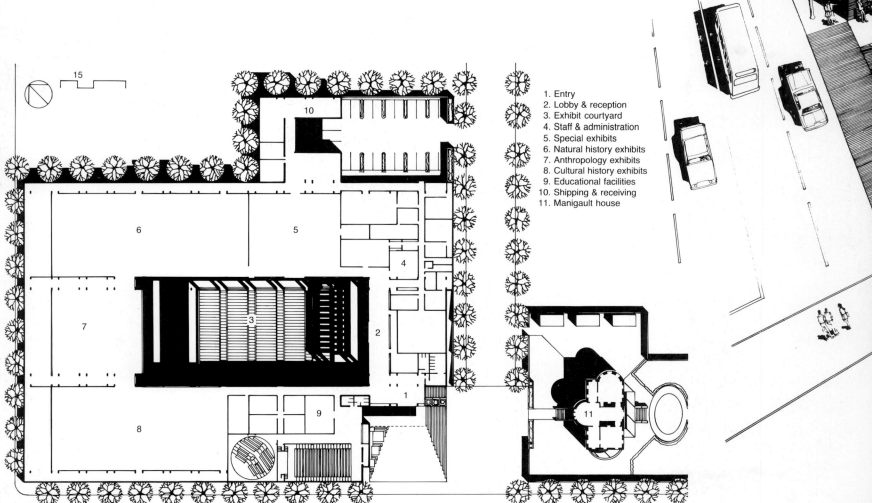

1. Entry
2. Lobby & reception
3. Exhibit courtyard
4. Staff & administration
5. Special exhibits
6. Natural history exhibits
7. Anthropology exhibits
8. Cultural history exhibits
9. Educational facilities
10. Shipping & receiving
11. Manigault house

# FEDERAL BUILDING, UNITED STATES COURTHOUSE

*Fort Lauderdale, Florida, 1976–1979*

This sheltered entrance becomes an interior court, arranged with planting and water flow. Open to the sky, its pedestrian walkways are sheltered from rain as well as sun. The building's interior office and court spaces are contained in four L-shaped tiers. The tops of several interior court spaces rise above the third-floor terraces.

The building's interior spaces are organized on a 5' × 5' planning module, that being a requirement of the owner, the U.S. General Services Administration. This module allows needed flexibility, the GSA being responsible for internal spatial configuration. One courtroom, for example, occupies a 30' × 40' space, another 40' × 60'. In studying the plan, one sees four spaces on the second-floor level that have high ceilings. Two of them are courtrooms, two are suitable for arbitration hearings.

The building has a gross area of 336,014 sf, including parking. Assignable (net) office spaces constitute 150,000 sf.

The Fort Lauderdale Federal Courts and Office Building represents William Morgan's architectural inclinations brought to a point of high resolution. In this work his desire for structural discipline, systems integration, clarity of form, spatial interplay, human scale, historic reference, and appropriate monumental expression achieves a level of distinct maturity.

The building occupies nearly all (90%) of a 2-acre site (255' × 356' = 90,780 sf). The building itself is a rectangle, measuring 231' × 351'. It has a level for parking, slightly below street level. Above that four stories rise to a height of 56'.

The below-grade parking level has space for 230 cars, as well as building service. It also has public elevator access points, one for building services in addition to people. A separate private elevator is provided for court judges, a normal requirement in court buildings. Vehicular access is from the north.

In addition to public access from the parking level, the building has a grand pedestrian entrance at its southeast corner. It is an entrance worthy of the best traditions of public buildings, assertively conveying a nobility of public service in behalf of the law. While grand in character it is equally human—even joyful—in scale.

## STRUCTURE

The structure consists of a concrete "tree," a concept used in the Police Administration Building in Jacksonville a few years earlier.

The 5' × 5' planning module is the basis of a still larger structural module of 30' × 30'. Column shafts, of concrete, are "cross" shaped, 32" × 32". They support a horizontal "branch" of concrete cantilevers consisting of four 10' × 10' coffers, the four constituting a 20' × 20' cantilevered-and-beamed canopy. The concrete canopy has a structural depth of 3'6", with 3' coffer recesses. Between the 20' × 20' canopies is a two-directional unobstructed space for mechanical systems. The coffers themselves are illuminated indirectly, casting a diffused interior light.

Federal Building-United States Courthouse

The only interruption to this system occurs in the large courtroom space on the second floor, where one "tree" is eliminated to avoid the obstruction of the space.

The floor system was poured on a plywood form-work base, jumbo-sized "pans" being used to form the coffers. Weighing 400 pounds each, they had to be positioned by cranes. There were 200 pan forms and 34 column forms used. This type of concrete construction, while having many benefits, required greater time and care in placing concrete than would ordinarily be the case. Overall cost savings, however, were substantial, 25 percent below budget.

The "trees" are deployed with complete geometric regularity, 8 "trees" north-south, 12 "trees" east-west. This gives a total of 96 "trees." The entire structure can also be regarded as a system of spatial cubes, each 30' × 30' in plan, for a total of 384 such cubes in four levels above grade.

In a sense, having established the "tree"-formed cubes, the design exercise consisted of subtracting cubes from the building, establishing a system of positive and negative spaces with a forest of concrete "trees." Morgan found a striking similarity of approach with the work of the Italian sculptor Arnoldo Pomodoro.

## MECHANICAL
The GSA specified that the level of energy consumption could not exceed 53,000 BTU / sf / year. Ample overhangs shading exterior glass helped achieve this level. By locating the garage just below grade, it was possible to bring natural light and ventilation into it, thereby avoiding a mechanical lighting and ventilating system for it.

## MATERIALS
Materials are exposed cast-in-place concrete with smooth finish, with infilling split faced masonry units with contrasting rough surface. The court is richly landscaped and has cascading pools.

## COST
GSA set a cost limit of $14,500,000. Actual cost was held below this, $10,800,000. The landscaping cost under $50,000.

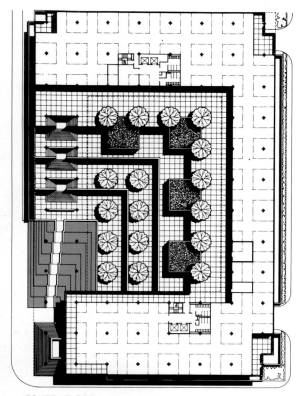

FOURTH FLOOR

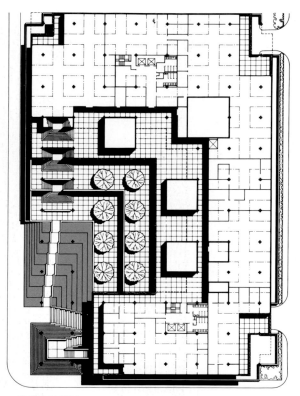

THIRD FLOOR

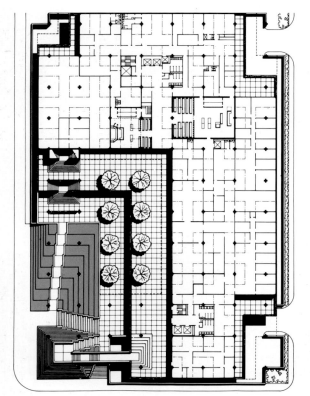

SECOND FLOOR

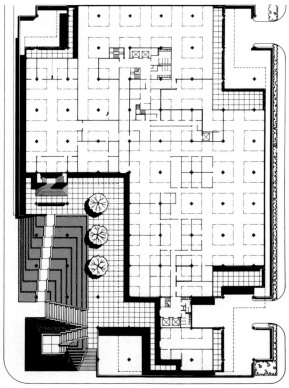

FIRST FLOOR

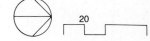

20

CLIENT: *General Services Administration, Region IV, Atlanta*
ASSOCIATED ARCHITECT: *Wright, Ferguson, Glasgow, and Schuster*
STRUCTURAL, MECHANICAL, AND ELECTRICAL ENGINEER: *H. J. Ross Associates*
LANDSCAPE ARCHITECT: *Stressau, Smith, and Stressau*
INTERIOR DESIGN: *Vida Stirbys Brown*
LIGHTING: *William Lam Associates*
ACOUSTICS: *Ranger Farrell and Associates*
FIRE SAFETY: *Rolf Jenson and Associates*
GRAPHIC DESIGN: *Dave Meyer and Associates*
CONTRACTOR: *Henry C. Beck Construction Management*

# ASSESSMENT

Just as Morgan's practice entered a period promising expansion and more challenging projects, the 1974 recession occurred, brought about by the oil crisis and price rise. Several projects were canceled. The Interama Amphitheater and the Norfolk Townpoint were the first victims. They were followed by the cancellation of the Perdue Office Building project, designed in the interval of work just presented.

Of the seven projects of this interval of work, the Dickinson house draws on an ancient architectural configuration—the pure prism elevated above the earth and set on a clean-sculpted earth podium. Among its historical counterparts is the Palace of the Governors at Uxmal (A.D. 800–900).

Of all of Morgan's projects none generated more publicity than the double-unit Atlantic Beach Dunehouses. Though tiny in size (750 sf in floor area, each), they demonstrated the possibility of achieving a sense of interior spaciousness not often found in far larger houses. Their most compelling feature, however, was the manner in which they were burrowed into their host sand dune. As to precedent, forerunner, resource, architectural issue—however one may wish to describe that—Morgan has made reference to two sources. One is the vestibule stairway of the Laurentian Library in Florence, designed by Michelangelo (1558). The other is the internal spatial arrangement of a modern submarine.

The Perdue Office Building has, certainly, to be reckoned one of the most unfortunate victims of the 1974 recession. Its landscape setting, the "Delmarva" peninsula of Delaware, Maryland, and Virginia, has been under con-

stant development pressure and could well have benefited from the design direction this building offered. It is a pity that it was not realized after the recovery from 1974.

With the Beach House significant advances in the handling of an earth-integrated pyramid structure were achieved. The crystalline organization of its plan recalls again that age-old architectural urge—to emulate the logic of nature's structures.

The Daniel Building in Jacksonville also explores one of architecture's more preoccupying challenges—the stepped terrace configuration. This type of building consists of totally open floors, which was largely possible to achieve here. But the building's use can be changed—possibly to that of a museum or a gallery. If so, all of its floors could be opened to full perimeter view. In the flow of Morgan's work it is significant, structurally, in its use of paired beams. This system, like the "trees," is a visually expressive means of integrating support structure with ceiling-borne mechanical systems. Paired columns accomplish the same purpose vertically. Further features of this building are its integration with a large parking structure and the possibility of converting that to office or exhibit space.

The Charleston Museum may possibly be seen as a bit of a warning to Morgan and to others who may at times be quick to apply a particular design notion, however useful elsewhere. The idea of an unobtrusive horizontal scheme came in answer to the idea of deferring, visually, to a handsome historical house. In doing that a park site was all but filled. The design selected—the project was

done in a competition—was a self-assured mass that acted in visual counterpoise to the house. The winning design proposed a 1:1 relationship with the old house, as well as leaving the park largely unbuilt, as a green urban open space. Morgan, out of an urge to defer far more to the old house, proposed a ½:1 relationship. But the cost of doing that was the cost of the park as a familiar type of urban open space—that is, one at ground level. Morgan proposed, instead, a rooftop space. It was not the same. Not all challenges are destined to be resolved. A significant source for the Charleston Museum project was the design for the Museum of History and Anthropology in Mexico City, by Pedro Ramírez Vasques (1968).

Last in this interval, the Federal Courthouse in Fort Lauderdale further explores the theme of the "trees," as first posed in the Jacksonville Police Administration Building. Here the "tree" tops are enlarged to 30' × 30'. And the conceptual arrangement of the Police Building—modular cells deployed around two connected interior spaces—yields to still another configuration. What we have in the courts building is, essentially, a series of uniform cubes of space composing a gigantic rectangular box—with selective cubes of space eliminated. This "subtractive architecture" results in a generous if not noble entrance space with distributed access to courts and offices. Morgan's references here are, again, to an Indian mound, specifically, the descending terraces of Falling Garden in St. Louis (A.D. 900–1450), but, even more telling, to the sculpture of the Italian Arnoldo Pomodoro.

This interval saw the full development of Morgan's essays into integrated systems. Paired columns and beams facilitate the integration of structural lighting, mechanical, electrical, and other building systems. This evolved from the first 27' × 27' "tree" system, later 30' × 30'. The paired beams and columns permit greater span in one direction, 60' in the Daniel Building. Paired beams and columns have often been used by Morgan in the Charleston Museum and other buildings, in both concrete and wood.

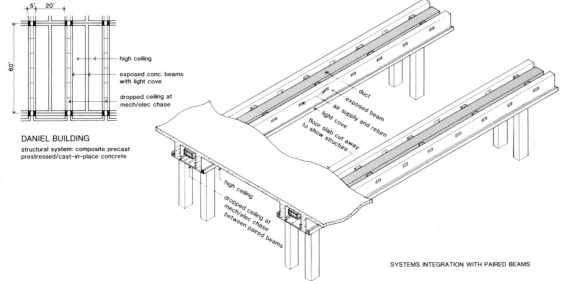

DANIEL BUILDING
structural system: composite precast prestressed/cast–in–place concrete

high ceiling
exposed conc. beams with light cove
dropped ceiling at mech/elec chase

duct
exposed beam
air supply and return
light cove
floor slab cut away to show structure

high ceiling
dropped ceiling at mech/elec chase between paired beams

SYSTEMS INTEGRATION WITH PAIRED BEAMS

SEA GARDENS

WATKINS RESIDENCE

FLORIDA STATE CONFERENCE CENTER

FOREST HOUSE

DISTRICT COURT OF APPEAL, FIRST DISTRICT

OCEANFRONT TOWNHOUSES

TREEHOUSE

1976–1980

# SEA GARDENS

*Seminole Beach, Florida, 1977–1979*

The significance of the Sea Gardens is as much in its site design as in the design of its component housing units.

Fifteen units are arranged in four clusters. Two of the four have three houses each, one cluster has four houses, and one cluster has five houses. All clusters are located on the western (inland) side of the site to allow the preservation of a primary sand dune as well as dense vegetation.

The houses are square in plan, 29′ × 29′, and three stories high. The square plan facilitates clustering, at the same time allowing variation in orientation. The lower floor in each house has sheltered parking and common living areas. The ten houses nearest the roadway have enclosed gardens. The upper floors of the units are bedrooms, three per unit. The houses range in size from 1,479 sf to 1,765 sf of interior living area.

## SITE

The site is 150′ wide by 550′ long, its long dimension oriented east-west. The eastern side of the site—the primary dune and dense vegetation—is left almost intact. A wood boardwalk gives access to the beach. Two wood sitting platforms atop the dune offer fine views of the ocean. Site density is 7.9 units per acre.

An especially ingenious aspect of the site design is the circular access driveway, 140′ in diameter. It gives access to all the units and also serves for emergency vehicle access with large turning radii, such as firetrucks.

In addition to the sheltered parking, the site provides parking for another sixteen automobiles, four at the entrance and twelve along the circular drive.

CLIENT: *Tore-King, Inc.*
STRUCTURAL ENGINEER: *H. W. Keister Associates*
MECHANICAL AND ELECTRICAL ENGINEER:
*Roy Turknett Engineers*
CONTRACTOR: *Demetree Builders*

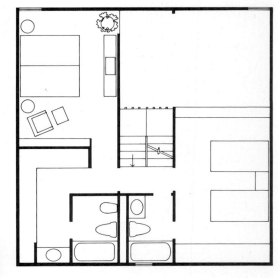

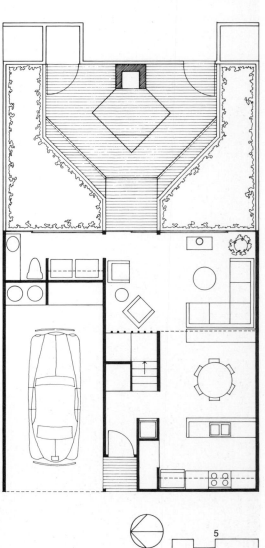

158

# WATKINS RESIDENCE

*Orange Park, Florida, 1977*

The seeming simplicity of the plan of this house belies its numerous subtleties. It is a plan worth careful study.

The requirements were to provide a house for a family of four, including two teenage girls. The elements of the house, on three levels, are indoor and outdoor family living spaces, private individual bedrooms, and a carefully tailored fit between site and structure.

The house is approached by automobile from the east. The approach road skirts the house on the north side, culminating in an entrance courtyard. The main living areas of the house are elevated to take advantage of a view of the St. Johns River in the distance.

The lower floor has an automobile entrance and sheltered parking. Access to the deck and

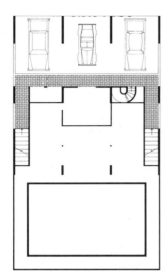 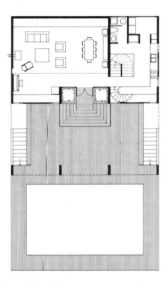 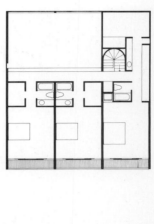

pool is via two flanking half flights of stairs. This is a convenient feature for entertaining large numbers of guests at a deck or pool party. A circular stair leads directly into the house, arriving at a most convenient point— the kitchen. The stair continues to the upper floor, minimizing through-house circulation. On this second level is a two-story living area, overlooked by a balcony, which leads to the daughters' bedrooms. The upper floor has three bedrooms, each with its own bathroom and balcony.

Glass areas are well shaded from the sun, as is the outdoor deck. One can well imagine the range of possibilities and conveniences in living here. There are community and privacy, the possibility of small or large group enter-tainment, the use of the outdoors in hot or rainy weather—and all in a setting of varied spaces.

The site is a rectangle, 100′ × 410′, oriented east-west. The house measures 43′10″ × 52′0″ overall and is 24′10″ high. The house contains 2,563 sf of enclosed living area. The pool has a 657-sf deck. The house is built of wood frame on a concrete slab. The pool has cedar decking. Vertical rough-sawn cedar is used as an interior and exterior finish. Interior floors are carpeted. Heating and cooling are by means of a heat pump.

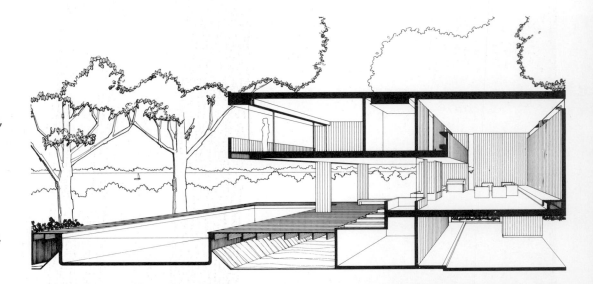

CLIENT: *Mr. and Mrs. Jesse Watkins*
STRUCTURAL ENGINEER: *H. W. Keister Associates*
MECHANICAL AND ELECTRICAL ENGINEER:
*Roy Turknett Engineers*
CONTRACTOR: *Watkins Construction Co.*

# FLORIDA STATE CONFERENCE CENTER
*Tallahassee, Florida, 1978–1982*

Located near the Tallahassee/Leon County Civic Center as well as the campus of Florida State University, this conference center was designed to serve a number of important functions.

First was a diversity of types of users—groups of up to four hundred persons for lecture-seminars, meetings of a small number of persons or many persons, and seminars of a dozen or two dozen persons. Type of conference and the number of participants covered a broad range. A second requirement was an atmosphere conducive to stimulating informal interaction and discussion. A third was the ability to accommodate several groups at the same time.

Such general objectives as well as particulars were identified by a special discussion with the client and by visits to several operating conference centers. The result was the design of a facility with a welcoming and relaxed atmosphere, where meeting spaces open onto informal interior and exterior gathering and strolling places.

The design program specified a large seminar room–auditorium for four hundred, a large dividable meeting room, a large dining room, a number of seminar rooms for groups of different sizes, administrative offices, and informal gathering spaces.

## SITE

The site is irregular in form, about 300′ × 400′, comprising 3.1 acres. It had some fine mature trees and an overall slope of 20′. The building is rectilinear in configuration, irregu-

lar in overall form. Its two stories contain 49,560 gross sf. The building occupies 39 percent of the site—30 percent for the structure, 9 percent for court, terraces, and walkways.

## BUILDING

The principal visitor entrance to the building is on the north, where a sheltered walkway extends to a vehicular entrance and car parking area. Another pedestrian entrance is from the east, via a series of stepped sitting enclosures leading into a central courtyard. There are two truck service points, one at the building's southwest corner, for serving the kitchen and large meeting rooms. A subsidiary truck dock at the northeast corner serves the needs of the seminar rooms.

A visitor entering via the principal entrance

1. Lobby
2. Courtyard
3. Registration
4. Auditorium
5. Meeting room
6. Dining-conference
7. Seminar room
8. Administration
9. Truck dock

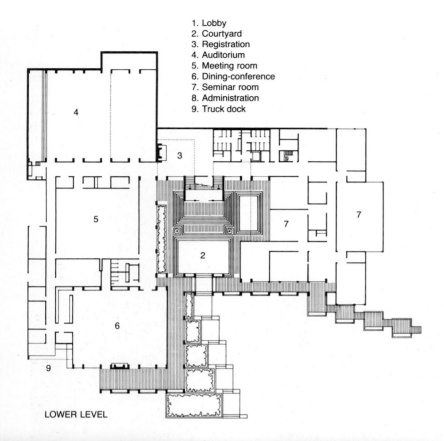

LOWER LEVEL

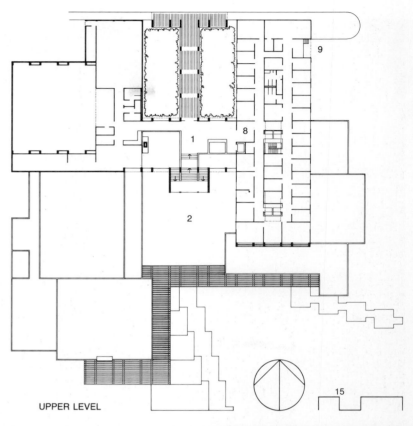

UPPER LEVEL

15

from the north arrives at the upper level of this two-story building. From there he or she enters a two-story reception area. Still on the upper level, administrative offices are found to the left. Most meeting rooms are on the lower level.

The eastern portion of the lower level contains the seminar rooms, nine in all. The western portion has the four-hundred-seat auditorium—seminar room, the dividable meeting room, and the dining area (which can also be used for meetings). All are grouped in a U around the court. Trellised walkways with seats extend informally from the court.

Both the dining room and the entrance area have fireplaces. The scale of the building is in keeping with that of nearby houses and a church. Its wood finish is in keeping with the relaxed character underlying the building's purpose—stimulating discourse.

## STRUCTURE
The building's structure is of particular interest: laminated wood beams, organized on an unusual module. This module operates in only an east-west sense, as a series of long and parallel bays. These bays are, alternately, 7'7" and 12'5" wide. The narrow bays serve as mechanical chases between beams.

## MECHANICAL
The building is cooled by a ground-water heat-exchanger system. The meeting and seminar rooms are heated and cooled by systems independent from the administrative offices'.

## COST
The building cost $2,822,943, including site work, or $56.96 / sf.

CLIENT: *Department of General Services, State of Florida, for the Board of Regents*
STRUCTURAL ENGINEER: *H. W. Keister Associates*
MECHANICAL AND ELECTRICAL ENGINEER: *Roy Turknett Engineers*
LANDSCAPE ARCHITECT: *Diversified Environmental Planning*
ACOUSTICS: *Christopher Jaffe*
GRAPHIC DESIGN: *Dave Meyer and Associates*
CONTRACTOR: *Winchester Construction Co.*

# FOREST HOUSE

*Gainesville, Florida, 1977–1979*

"We have become so dazzled by all the new materials at our disposal that we forget that the first and most abundant building material was earth itself." So commented William Morgan about this house, whose form derives, in large part, from the use of earth as a building material. He continued, "The builders of prehistoric America knew that earth is a strong, suitable building material, weather resistant and easily moved. They did the obvious and built with the land's most abundant resource."

The Forest House advances, still further, Morgan's efforts to develop architectural form as earth form, to ally geometric discipline with function, and, all the while, to deal with the essentials of architecture—materials, light, space, proportion, mechanics.

The site is an oak-filled 56-acre tract. The house is approached from the west by means of a long drive through the woods. The house itself consists of two flat-topped pyramids oriented on a north-south spine. The two pyramids are connected by a covered walkway, which serves as an entrance portico for visitors, who arrive on the portico's western side. The owners drive their cars to the garage structure, the northern and smaller pyramid.

The southern pyramid is the residence itself. Entering from the portico on its northern end, one first encounters a sky-lit planted vestibule. Ahead is a blank free-standing wall surface, the rear of a fireplace. One goes to the right or left of it and, in doing so, arrives in a spacious central living room. It is lit by a south-facing clerestory. Ahead is a wood deck and screen-covered pool.

Flanking the living room are two L-shaped configurations of rooms. The group to the left (east) is the owners' bedroom, bath, and dressing areas and a guest room—study. To the right (west) are the kitchen and dining areas, a guest room, and a bath.

The east and west corners of the pyramids have vertical "light scoops," which bring daylight to the owners' bathroom (east) and the kitchen (west). The study and guest rooms receive lateral light from the planted entrance vestibule. The prismatic plan-form of the fireplace is recalled in smaller form in six symmetrically disposed display cabinets, in which the owners' collection of artifacts can be viewed.

The deck and pool are accessible from the owners' bedroom, the living room, and the

dining area. Doors between the deck and pool and their interior spaces can be closed during rainy or otherwise uncomfortable weather, or they can be left open during rainshowers, as is done in porches in this area.

The structure of the house is reinforced concrete walls, earth mounds, and wood frame roof. It could hardly be a simpler idea, or a more elegant one.

CLIENT: *Dr. and Mrs. Joshua C. Dickinson, Jr.*
STRUCTURAL ENGINEER: *H. W. Keister Associates*
MECHANICAL AND ELECTRICAL ENGINEER: *Roy Turknett Engineers*
LANDSCAPE ARCHITECT: *Diversified Environmental Planning*
CONTRACTOR: *T. J. Kimbrell*

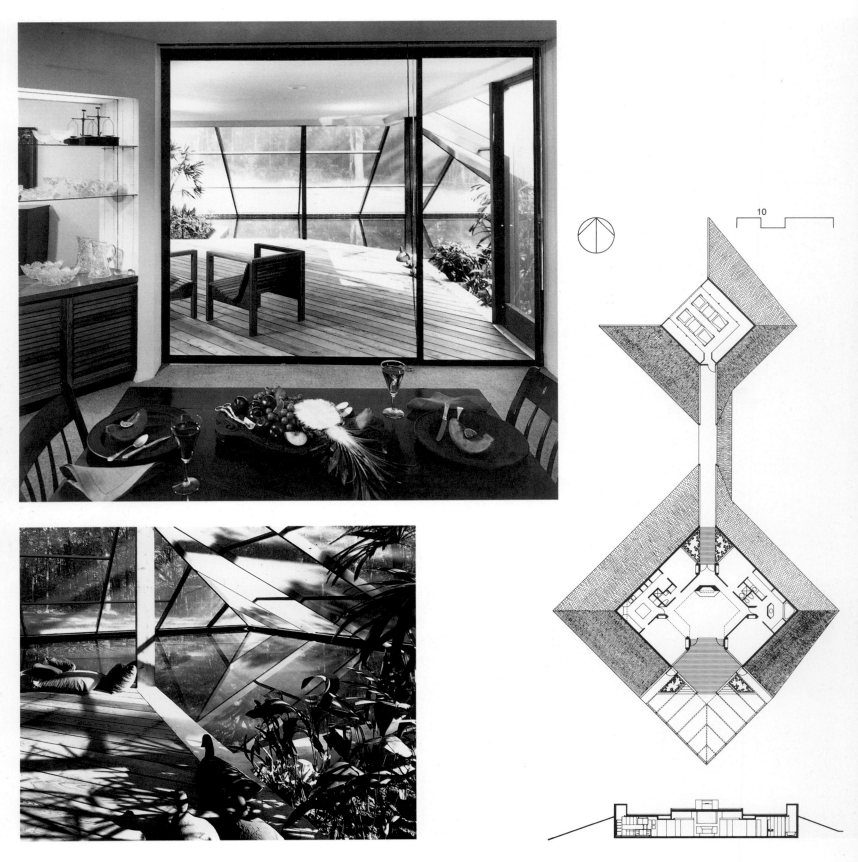

# DISTRICT COURT OF APPEAL, FIRST DISTRICT

*Tallahassee, Florida, 1978–1981*

The site for Florida's First District Court of Appeal borders the grounds of the State Capitol and is within sight of the Florida State University School of Law. In interviewing the twelve judges who were to use the building, Morgan found a complete range of views regarding an appropriate architectural character. Perhaps the most moderate view was expressed by the judge who remarked that the building "should look like a courthouse." But a keynote was struck by one judge's response to a query by Morgan, who asked him what his favorite building was. "The Parthenon" was the judge's reply. To that and several other references, this building owes its character. In fact the building owes more to the proportions of the temple of Paestum, with its drumlike columns.

Also among the references is the foursquare tradition of northern Florida courthouses generally. Those buildings are placed in the centers of their sites, convey a sense of public purpose, and have a sense of public accessibility. The State Capitol complex buildings themselves make extensive use of white-painted brick, which Morgan used for this building.

The building itself has a basement and three floors. The basement has storage and building support service spaces, including mechanical rooms.

The first floor has, as its focus, a central courtroom. It rises two stories (24') in height and has a central lantern, which extends 40' to a rooftop skylight and admits daylight. Its interior finish is wood paneling. Three judges normally preside, but by moving nearby furnishings it is possible to accommodate a larger number.

The first floor also has a clerk's office, a law library, a commons room, and a conference room.

The second level has twelve suites of judges' chambers, each with three rooms. Additional space on this and a third floor set back from the roof's edge accommodates a support staff of sixty persons.

## SITE
The site measures 300' × 400', its long dimension being east-west. The site also slopes upward about 25' to the east. It is bordered by mature oak, magnolias, and pecans.

The court building sits at the center of the site and can be approached on foot by a broad and welcoming entrance plaza. There are four parking areas at the site's corners. There is a service drive between the entrance plaza and the building, under a connecting bridge.

## STRUCTURE
Paired beams and columns on an 18' × 36' module form a series of ceiling channels and coffers, in which mechanical systems are integrated. The structure is made of reinforced concrete. The exterior columns are enclosed in 4'-diameter brick cylinders, which are painted white. The building measures 130' × 130'.

## MECHANICAL
Cooling is provided by a central chilled-water system utilizing a cooling tower and a 75-ton centrifugal chiller. Heating is provided by means of a 15-HP gas / oil-fired hot-water heater. Central air-handling units supply air to variable volume boxes, which are controlled by zone thermostats. The systems have an economizer cycle, which allows the use of outside air, conditions permitting.

A 120/208, 3-phase, 4-wire system has a total connected load of 450 KVA and an estimated demand of 350 KVA. Fluorescent strips in coves provide indirect lighting throughout at the required 45 esi footcandle level within the energy budget of 2 watts / sf.

## COST
The building cost $3,105,000, including site work, landscaping, and courtroom furnishings. Its gross area is 48,500 sf—16,900 sf below ground, 31,600 sf above. Cost was $64.07 / sf.

FIRST FLOOR

SECOND FLOOR

THIRD FLOOR

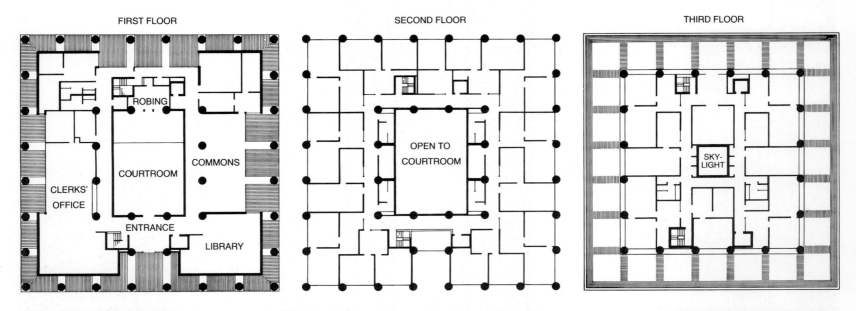

ROBING

COURTROOM

COMMONS

CLERKS' OFFICE

ENTRANCE

LIBRARY

OPEN TO COURTROOM

SKY-LIGHT

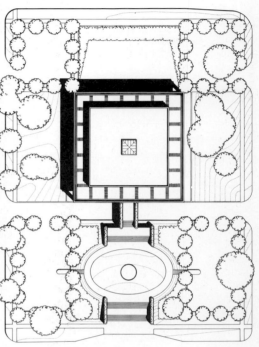

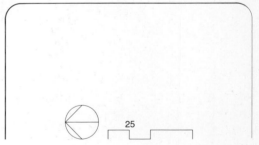

25

CLIENT: *State of Florida, Department of General Services*
STRUCTURAL ENGINEER: *H. W. Keister Associates*
MECHANICAL AND ELECTRICAL ENGINEER:
*Roy Turknett Engineers*
LANDSCAPING AND CIVIL ENGINEER: *Diversified Environmental Planning*
INTERIOR DESIGN: *Carlson-Deison*
LIGHTING: *William Lam Associates*
ACOUSTICS: *Christopher Jaffe*
CONTRACTOR: *Martin-Johnson, Inc.*

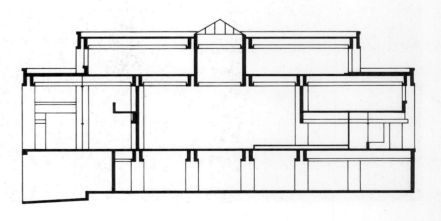

# OCEANFRONT TOWNHOUSES

*Atlantic Beach, Florida, 1979–1982*

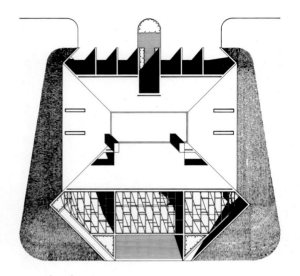

The beach-front site of this residence of three dwelling units is normally occupied by single houses on 50'-wide lots. The owners had a 100'-wide site and wished to build three residences, one for themselves and two for sale.

Each unit was to have three bedrooms, high energy efficiency, through ventilation, minimum maintenance, privacy, oceanfront living, maximum hurricane resistance, and ocean views. In addition, the view of the ocean from an adjoining inland lot was to be preserved.

A preliminary design explored the possibility of siting the owners' house on the northern end of the site, with the two other units built as a duplex on the southern end. But the pyramid concept enabled all three to be combined in one structure while satisfying all requirements and adding several advantages.

The central unit is the owners' and has three levels. It is entered on the west side through a shared six-car sheltered carport. The ground level has a high-ceiling living-dining area and an entrance and kitchen area with normal ceiling height. This entire area opens onto a sheltered deck and screened swimming pool. The level below is for utility and storage of beach paraphernalia. The upper level has two bedrooms, a studio-sleeping area, and baths. The upper level occupies part of the upper areas of each of the two side units.

These side units are identical in plan, being "mirror images" of each other. Each has its own entrance, a high-level atrium. Each has two levels. The lower level has one bedroom, a living room, and a high-ceiling kitchen-

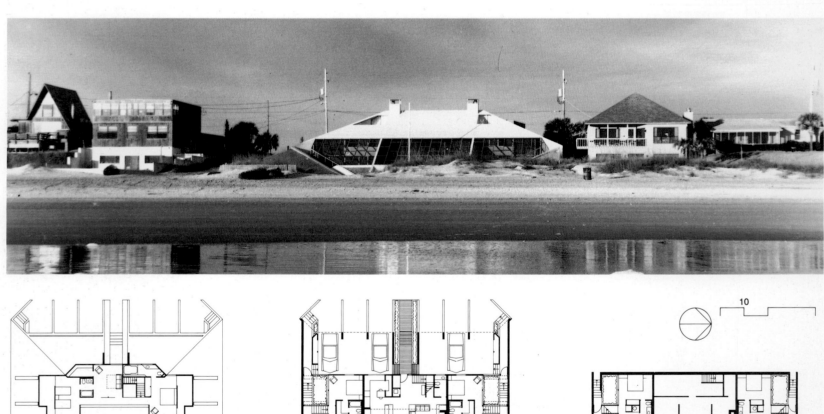

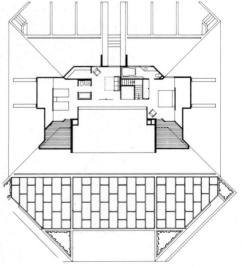

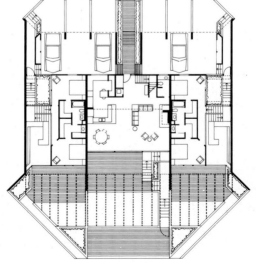

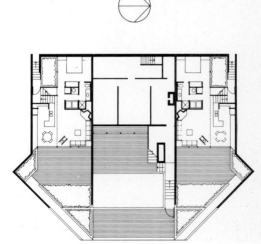

10

dining area. This level opens onto a screened deck. The entire level is below grade and has a ramped accessway to the beach. The upper level has two bedrooms, baths, and storage.

The degree of privacy in so compact a structure is remarkable. The upper-level bedrooms of the owners' unit have private decks located above the screened decks of the two side units. Their placement in relation to the roof line blocks views between the two.

The structure is concrete slab on grade, with concrete walls separating units on the lower levels and acting as retaining walls for the side berms. The remaining structure is wood frame and plywood. The roof is a white elastomeric membrane. The berm was formed from excavation material, balancing cut and fill.

CLIENT: *Mr. and Mrs. George M. Goodloe*
STRUCTURAL ENGINEER: *H. W. Keister Associates*
MECHANICAL AND ELECTRICAL ENGINEER:
*Roy Turknett Engineers*
CONTRACTOR: *E. Vaughn Rivers, Inc.*

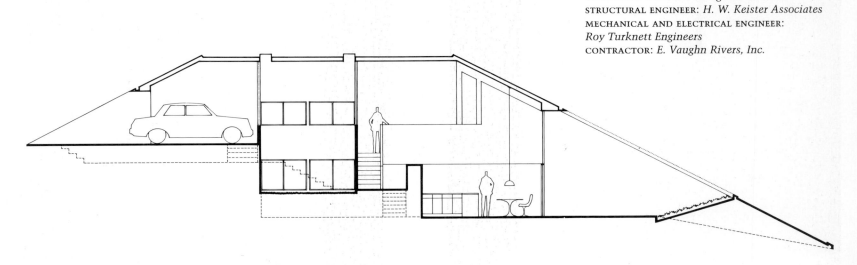

# TREEHOUSE

*Atlantic Beach, Florida, 1979–1983*

Intended as a prototype for high-density residential development, this design addresses the commonplace issue of providing an ocean view from properties near the ocean but not fronting directly on a beach view. The site of the treehouse is just to the west of the site of the Oceanfront Townhouses, the project previously described. The low pyramidal form of the Oceanfront Townhouses makes an ocean view from the treehouse possible.

But the idea of a treehouse is, in itself, one of mankind's most ancient urges, emanating from the experience of animal ancestors and recapitulating itself in the years of childhood.

The treehouse is three stories high and has the simplest possible geometry. It sits on a lot 100' × 156'8". The house is 20' × 20' on the lower two floors, 28' × 28' on the upper floor.

The ground floor has parking for two cars and the house entrance. The second floor has two children's bedrooms. The upper floor has a kitchen-dining-living area and the parents' bedroom. This level also has a fireplace and sheltered balcony. The location of the children's rooms on the second floor assures privacy for the parents.

The house has through ventilation and seldom requires air conditioning. The structure is wood frame. Exterior walls are cedar siding on plywood. Interior ceilings are exposed wood; walls are painted gypsum. The roof is elastomeric roofing on foam insulation, sloped for drainage. Heating and cooling are by means of a heat pump. The plan layout is based on a 10' × 10' module.

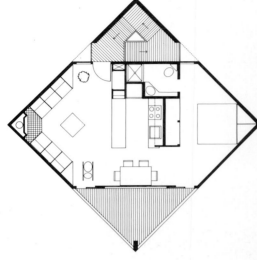

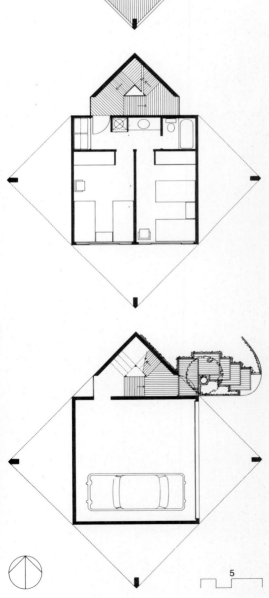

5

CLIENT: *Morgan Properties*
STRUCTURAL ENGINEER: *H. W. Keister Associates*
MECHANICAL AND ELECTRICAL ENGINEER:
*Roy Turknett Engineers*
CONTRACTOR: *Grider-Riechmann Contractors*

# ASSESSMENT

Though a period of relatively small projects, this interval of Morgan's work produced several masterful jewels. In two instances—the Oceanfront Townhouses and the Treehouse, Morgan was developer / owner as well as architect. This very old but newly rediscovered aspect of practice enabled him to fill the inevitable lulls between commissions.

The Sea Gardens project is significant for its integration of buildings with site, the site largely generating the position and deployment of structures.

The Watkins residence is a masterful resolution of elementary urges to organizational clarity seen in Morgan's earliest efforts.

The Florida State Conference Center succeeds in a quiet deployment of masses on a sloped site, providing at the same time a place that stimulates meeting and exchange of ideas, formally as well as informally.

The Forest House, surely, is one of Morgan's jewels. Its logic of plan and its appropriateness to its site speak clearly to all—in plan as much as in photographs. It is the kind of seemingly simple yet highly sophisticated architecture that all designers aspire to produce.

The District Court of Appeal recalls a classicism long associated with orderly government. It has a degree of stateliness but, at the same time, a highly appropriate scale, its site being alongside other state government buildings. Its reference source is, of course, the classical Greek temple form.

The Oceanfront Townhouses, combining three dwelling units into one pyramidal form, is ingenious in its plan and an exemplary complement to its dune site. Like the Perdue Office Building this project, fortunately realized, deserves to be taken as a model—in this case, potentially an example for design and for capital investment.

Last in this group, the Treehouse is, as much as any of Morgan's designs, a little gem. Its simple form and clarity of plan are evidence that the tenets of modern architecture, as practiced in this country in the last decades, are as much a gift as anything history has known. If any reference is appropriate here it is not so much in architecture as it is in an old Quaker song, given finer form by the American composer Aaron Copland. The words are, "'Tis a gift to be simple . . . 'tis a gift to be free."

In this same period Morgan completed his research work on the Indian mound structures that had fascinated him for so many years.

With the help of grants from the National Endowment for the Arts and the Graham Foundation for Advanced Studies in the Fine Arts, he assimilated information on some four hundred mound sites. Of these eighty-two were selected for presentation in his book *Prehistoric Architecture in the Eastern United States* (MIT Press, 1980). The book is a model of research methodology from an architect's viewpoint, one from which archaeology in general has long benefited.

NEIMAN-MARCUS

THREE ELECTRIC SUBSTATIONS

WESTINGHOUSE ELECTRIC CORPORATION,
 STEAM TURBINE-GENERATOR DIVISION,
 WORLD HEADQUARTERS

ELECTRONIC DATA SYSTEMS HEADQUARTERS

SCHEININGER CLINIC

CREEK HOUSE

MESA HOUSING

1980–1982

# NEIMAN-MARCUS

*Fort Lauderdale, Florida, 1980–1982*

Paraphrasing Louis Kahn's famous remark, a branch department store probably "wants to be" a box—from a massing standpoint, at least. It is, after all, a self-contained enclosure providing a maximum of flexible space, open interior circulation, serviceability, and access. A box containing several floors with easy accessibility and serviceability is the answer. But there is a bit more to it, and that bit is significant.

A department store, as an object in the landscape, must also have a personality, an identity. It must be recognizable from a distance, and its entrance point (or points) must be clearly discernable. Its appearance must register clearly to a passing motorist, a driver searching for a parking space, and a shopper-pedestrian approaching on foot.

With all that, the spirit of its purpose deserves expression. And it is here that Morgan made a special design contribution. Reflecting on the memorial to Karl Liebknecht and Rosa Luxemburg designed in 1926 by Ludwig Miës van der Rohe, Morgan saw in its massing an expression of a future filled with possibility, its massing hovering and poised to suggest something not yet present, a bridge from the present to the future, a suggestion of hopes and possibilities yet to be fulfilled. All that is a poetic and entirely valid view of what the acquisition of material goods plays in our lives.

At the same time, Morgan's exterior treatment of the building is a response to the articulating Florida sunshine. And on the light-hearted side, the traylike boxlike configuration suggests the piling of gift boxes one atop another. The layering of greenery has an obvious association with Florida's vegetation.

Like some works of literature, this work of architecture can be appreciated on several levels—philosophical, whimsical, response to light, recollection of setting.

The building has two stories, placed above ground-level parking for one hundred cars. It measures 155′ × 265′ and contains 80,000 gross sf. Its structure is concrete, arranged in 32′8″ × 46′8″ bays. The surface material is exposed smooth-finish concrete, split-face concrete masonry units, and planting. The interior was designed by firms specializing in store interiors and lighting.

The building is entered from below from the parking level or laterally on the first floor from an adjacent shopping mall. Either way, persons arrive in a full-building-height atrium, which is also skylighted by clerestories.

The building cost $4,535,000, not including interior floor and wall finishes or store fixtures.

CLIENT: *Neiman-Marcus Co.*
STRUCTURAL, MECHANICAL, AND ELECTRICAL
ENGINEER: *H. J. Ross Associates*
LANDSCAPE ARCHITECT: *Stressau, Smith, and Stressau*
INTERIOR DESIGN: *Warneke / LeMaire*
LIGHTING: *Ray Grenald*
COST CONTROL: *Cibis*
CONTRACTOR: *Whiting-Turner Contracting Co.*

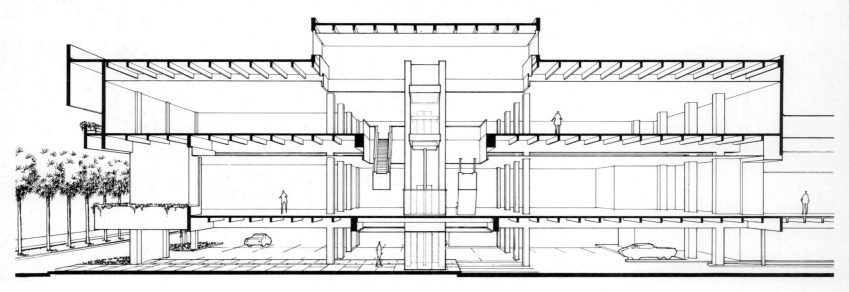

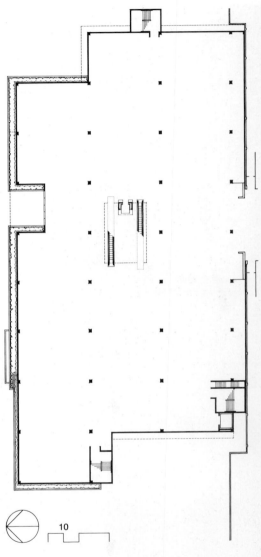

# THREE ELECTRIC SUBSTATIONS

*Jacksonville, Florida, 1980–1983*

In the early 1980s the Jacksonville Electric Authority undertook a major program to improve and enlarge the area's electrical distribution system. Included in that effort was the creation of three substations. Each was to be fully serviceable and environmentally compatible.

The first of these, the Church Street Substation, was completed in 1982 at a cost of $605,000. It was built in a blighted area. The corners of the 220' × 220' site were treated in such a way as to be usable as landscaped play spaces, the paving sloped for skateboarding. The enclosing wall is a circle of rough-textured cement masonry units, to deter graffiti as well as scaling. The interior is a simple and functional layout, the large radius circular roadway accommodating flatbed trucks needed to transport transformers.

The Main Street Substation was completed in 1983 at a cost of $648,000. Its site was rectangular, its enclosing wall an oval. Its interior layout and the treatment of its corners were similar to those of the Church Street Substation. Its surrounding wall was built of red brick, with pilasters and cornice. The reason for this was to respect and extend the character of its setting, a residential area of brick houses with a general motif of pilasters and cornices.

The Water Street Substation was completed in 1984 at a cost of $992,000. Its site is in downtown Jacksonville, across the street from the Daniel Building. It contains four separate elements—a small existing substation, new outdoor transformers, new interior transformer equipment that requires an overhead traveling crane, and parking for service vehicles. The exterior treatment of this substation derives from its proximity to the state office building. It has both an enclosing wall and a trellis roof, composed on a double-column and double-beam module derived directly from the system of the state office building. The trellis was included because the facility is visible from above from both present and future high-rise buildings.

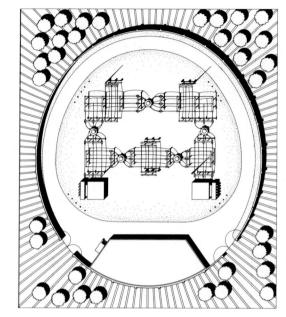

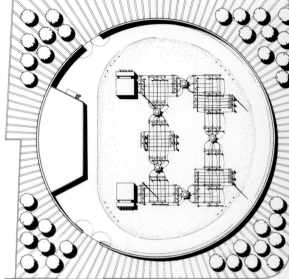

MAIN STREET SUBSTATION 15 CHURCH STREET SUBSTATION

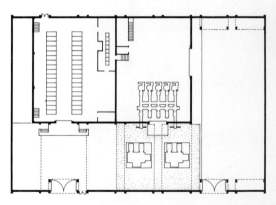

WATER STREET SUBSTATION

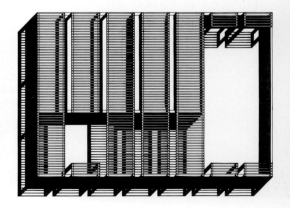

10

197

CLIENT: *Jacksonville Electric Authority*
STRUCTURAL ENGINEER: *H. W. Keister Associates*
MECHANICAL AND ELECTRICAL ENGINEER:
*Roy Turknett Engineers*
LANDSCAPE ARCHITECT: *Diversified Environmental
Planning*
CONTRACTORS:
*Church Street: M. E. Elkins Co. (1982)*
*Main Street: Melrose Construction Co. (1983)*
*Water Street: D. Coleman, Inc. (1984)*

# WESTINGHOUSE ELECTRIC CORPORATION, STEAM TURBINE-GENERATOR DIVISION, WORLD HEADQUARTERS

*Orlando, Florida, 1980–1983*

The design of this headquarters facility was guided by the following objectives:

1. Utilization of the site so as to have minimum environmental impact.
2. Open and accessible work atmosphere to facilitate employee communication and interaction.
3. Maximum daylighting of interior work spaces and perimeter offices.
4. Visual reduction of long interior corridors.
5. Integration of the building's structural, mechanical, and lighting systems.

## SITE

The Westinghouse site occupies 30 acres of a 400-acre development 10 miles east of Orlando. The focus of the site plan is Lake Ebby. The forested site was a former pasture. The site has a 25' slope to the lake. A curved approach drive brings visitors to a 130'-diameter grassed circle centered on the axis of the building, the center itself being the visitor entrance. Employee parking areas flank the main entrance.

The visitor entrance is on the building's second-floor level. Just outside the circular visitor drive and behind two flanking berms are two truck docks for building servicing. The employee parking areas slope one-story downward. Six employee entrances are located on the first-floor level.

## BUILDING

The building has the shape of a segment of a curved ring, its axial radius of curvature being 440'. The building measures 163'6" × 612'6" and contains 257,500 sf. It is composed of five symmetrical segments, the end pair being two stories high, the adjoining pair three stories, and the central segment four stories. The building is able to accommodate a staff of between 750 and 900 employees.

The central portion of the building houses a computer center, a cafeteria, and administrative offices on the upper level. The flanking offices house engineering research and marketing.

The four-story segment has a full atrium, its ends having glass-enclosed elevators. The central areas of the remaining segments contain support service spaces and are punctured by vertical stair spaces.

The four floors are staggered outward to shade exterior fenestration. A system of horizontal elements also contributes to fenestration shading against direct sunlight and

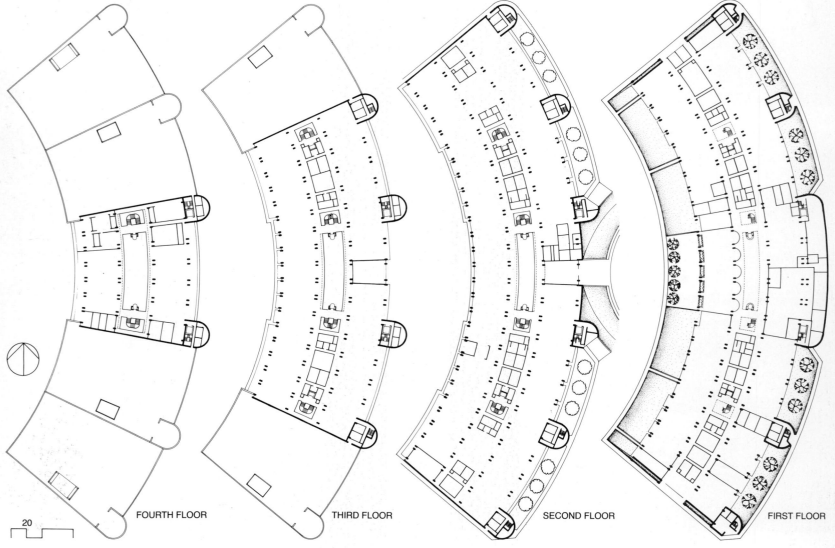

FOURTH FLOOR THIRD FLOOR SECOND FLOOR FIRST FLOOR

20

reflects diffused light to interiors. In the central segment atrium, the staggering allows more clerestory light to reach lower floors.

## STRUCTURE

Here again Morgan used a paired column and post system to facilitate integration among structure, lighting, and mechanical components. The floor-to-ceiling height is 11'6". The paired column and beam system is 17'6" × 44', the space between the paired structural elements being 5'. The beams and the structural slab are post-tensioned concrete. The curve of the building's plan-form is uniform for uniformity of forming. Exterior walls are white painted brick.

## MECHANICAL

The HVAC system consists of two 295-ton water-cooled centrifugal chillers supplied from two cooling towers. Local air handling units supply cooled air to interior zones through variable air volume boxes and to perimeter zones through fan terminal units. The building uses 35,000 BTU / sf annually.

The building has a 480/277 volt, 3-phase, 4-wire wye electric system. Two 3,000-amp switchboards can each supply two-thirds of the building load. This system serves all motor and power loads, as well as lighting. Step-down transformers are used for receptacles, task lighting, and incidental equipment.

Lighting is provided by continuous-strip fluorescent fixtures with energy efficient ballasts in recessed coves with parabolic louver lenses. A low-voltage microcomputer controls lighting level.

## COST

The building cost $14,880,000, or $57.82 / sf. This cost included site work and landscaping but not a movable partition system or special interior finishes.

CLIENT: *Westinghouse Electric Corporation, Power Generation Group*
STRUCTURAL ENGINEER: *Tilden, Lobnitz, and Cooper, Inc.*
MECHANICAL AND ELECTRICAL ENGINEER: *Roy Turknett Engineers*
CIVIL ENGINEER: *Richard P. Clarson and Associates*
LANDSCAPE ARCHITECT: *Herbert / Halback, Inc.*
INTERIOR DESIGN: *Interspace, Inc.*
LIGHTING: *William Lam Associates*
ACOUSTICS: *Christopher Jaffe*
CONTRACTOR: *Scandia, Inc.*

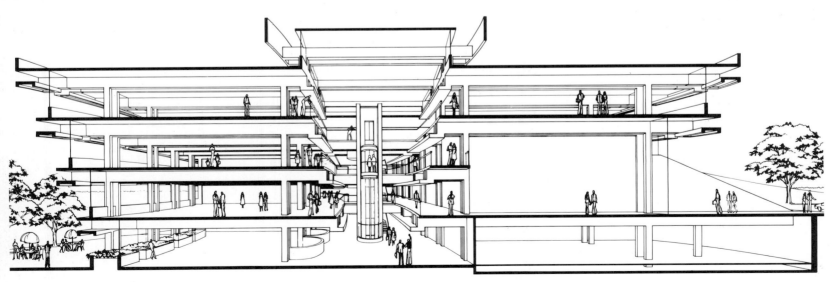

207

# ELECTRONIC DATA SYSTEMS HEADQUARTERS (project)

*Plano, Texas, 1980–1981*

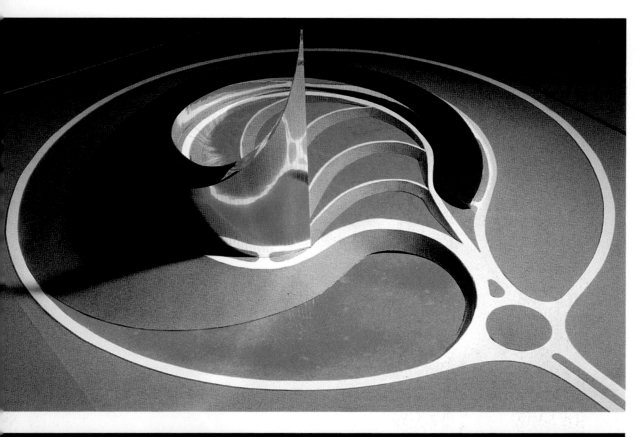

This project explores the possibility of utilizing a rising spiral as the basis of form for a headquarters office building. The site was the highest hill in a rural area. The building would consolidate the several functions of EDS into a single center. The facility was to be built in stages. The first, shown here, would have 915,000 sf, the ultimate facility 1,760,000 sf. The surrounding site was, otherwise, to be developed commercially. A nearby expressway was to be depressed, providing fill for the design's berm. The design was produced in an invited competition.

The entire building was to be set within a 1,500'-diameter circular roadway. Within that was a 950'-diameter roadway adjoining the building's outer edge. Between the two roadways the earth was to be banked up. The inner roadway would rise, consequently, its highest point being at the building's entry. The berm would also cover the building's lower parking floors. The spiral would begin as a one-story building, rising to a height of 600'. It would be visible from the Dallas–Fort Worth Regional Airport, around 20 miles away.

The interior court, a not quite complete circle, was to consist of five rising levels of pools. In plan these would have a pattern reminiscent of a conch shell in cross section. Their area was to be 47 acres.

The entire first-stage building (915,000 sf) was to include parking for 2,767 cars. The first-stage office area was to be 805,000 sf. In a later stage of development some of the structural parking could be converted to climate-controlled office space for computers. Interior parking would be shifted to the surface, outdoors. A shuttle bus would take workers from parking to offices.

Façades were to have been clad in reflective glass. The structural system was to be an economical system of concrete prestressed and precast beams spanning 48' and resting on paired columns in which ducts would be located. This would allow a low floor-to-floor height.

The 1981 cost was estimated at $83,000,000.

CLIENT: *H. Ross Perot*

208

# SCHEININGER CLINIC

*Jacksonville, Florida, 1981–1982*

This suburban medical clinic is located in an oak forest. It specializes in the treatment of obesity, which requires examination rooms and spaces for counseling, group discussion, exercise, and instructional lecturing.

The site measures 200′ × 250′. An approach roadway from the south leads to parking areas as well as patient and service entrances.

The building is square in plan, 66′ × 66′. At each of the corners is a 27′-diameter circular garden. The entire one-story plan, including gardens, is surrounded by an earth berm. Daylight is admitted laterally at the four corners and vertically at the building's center by nine skylights. The area of the building is 3,783 sf, of the four circular gardens 2,292 sf.

Patients enter on the south side, arrive at a reception desk, and proceed to the east wait-ing room. The waiting room is conducive to informal discussion, which is quite helpful in the treatment of obesity. The reception area adjoins an interior work and records area. The west waiting room is used for bill paying. Patients also wait there while prescriptions are filled. The staff enters the building from the east.

The center of the building has rooms for support activities—exercise, examination, storage. On the west is a lecture-demonstration room, on the east a service and diet preparation area. The northern part of the building has consultation and examination rooms, as well as a staff lounge.

Sunlight, filtered through the oak trees, reflects off the curved surfaces of the garden walls. The berms reduce air-conditioning load.

CLIENT: *Dr. David M. Scheininger*
STRUCTURAL ENGINEER: *H. W. Keister Associates*
MECHANICAL AND ELECTRICAL ENGINEER:
*Roy Turknett Engineers*
LANDSCAPE ARCHITECT: *Diversified Environmental
Planning*
CONTRACTOR: *Newman Construction Co.*

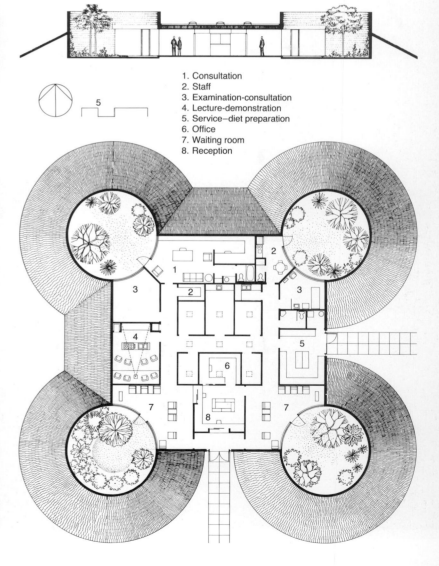

1. Consultation
2. Staff
3. Examination-consultation
4. Lecture-demonstration
5. Service—diet preparation
6. Office
7. Waiting room
8. Reception

# CREEK HOUSE (project)

*Austin, Texas, 1982–1984*

The site for this house was a 320-acre area in the Hill Country of Texas. A creek undercut a limestone ledge. The residence would have been located above the ledge, recessed into the hillside. Approaching visitors would have forded a creek, passing through a baffled entry to a forecourt filled with the sound of gently cascading water.

The owner wanted a house very much suited to the idiom of Texas climate and living. To draw on historic precedents of architecture in this climate, the client and the architect visited the Hill Country, the Davis Mountains, and Fort Leaton at Presidio, all in Texas. To absorb the Spanish heritage of Texas, they also traveled to Seville and to the Alhambra in Granada, Spain.

In the Creek House, the sound of gently falling water would have filled the air. The sound and motion of the water would be "scaled down" in the more private parts of the house, with a silent reflecting pool alongside the master bedroom suite. All water pools would be interconnected with channels, all ultimately flowing into the natural creek below the house.

The house itself was to have 7,000 sf of air-conditioned space, 4,000 sf of enclosed non-air-conditioned space, and 5,000 sf of conservatory and greenhouse area. The house would be about 386' long on a north-south axis and about 78' wide, east-west.

The northern end of the house was to be an automobile courtyard entry adjoining service elements: servants' quarters, kitchen, laundry, and so on. A dog kennel and dog runs were to be on the west. The next section of the house would be the main living area and have the form of a U. It would contain a library-terrace, a dining area, a living room, and the owners' master bedroom suite. The U would open onto an enclosed terraced garden and pool area.

The southern end of the house was to be the master bedroom suite, overlooking a quiet pool, at the end of which would be a studio.

The materials of the house were to be native limestone bearing walls with wood frame roof.

The project had to be abandoned when the Texas State Highway Department announced that the land would have to be appropriated for construction of a new highway.

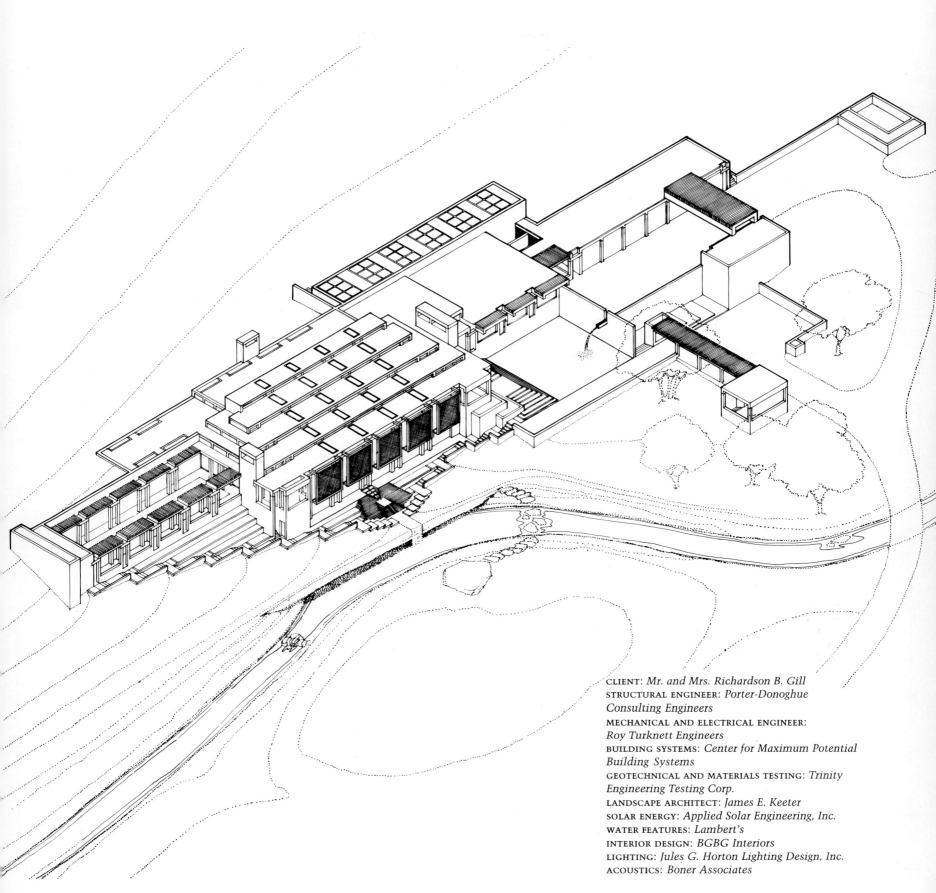

CLIENT: *Mr. and Mrs. Richardson B. Gill*
STRUCTURAL ENGINEER: *Porter-Donoghue Consulting Engineers*
MECHANICAL AND ELECTRICAL ENGINEER: *Roy Turknett Engineers*
BUILDING SYSTEMS: *Center for Maximum Potential Building Systems*
GEOTECHNICAL AND MATERIALS TESTING: *Trinity Engineering Testing Corp.*
LANDSCAPE ARCHITECT: *James E. Keeter*
SOLAR ENERGY: *Applied Solar Engineering, Inc.*
WATER FEATURES: *Lambert's*
INTERIOR DESIGN: *BGBG Interiors*
LIGHTING: *Jules G. Horton Lighting Design, Inc.*
ACOUSTICS: *Boner Associates*

215

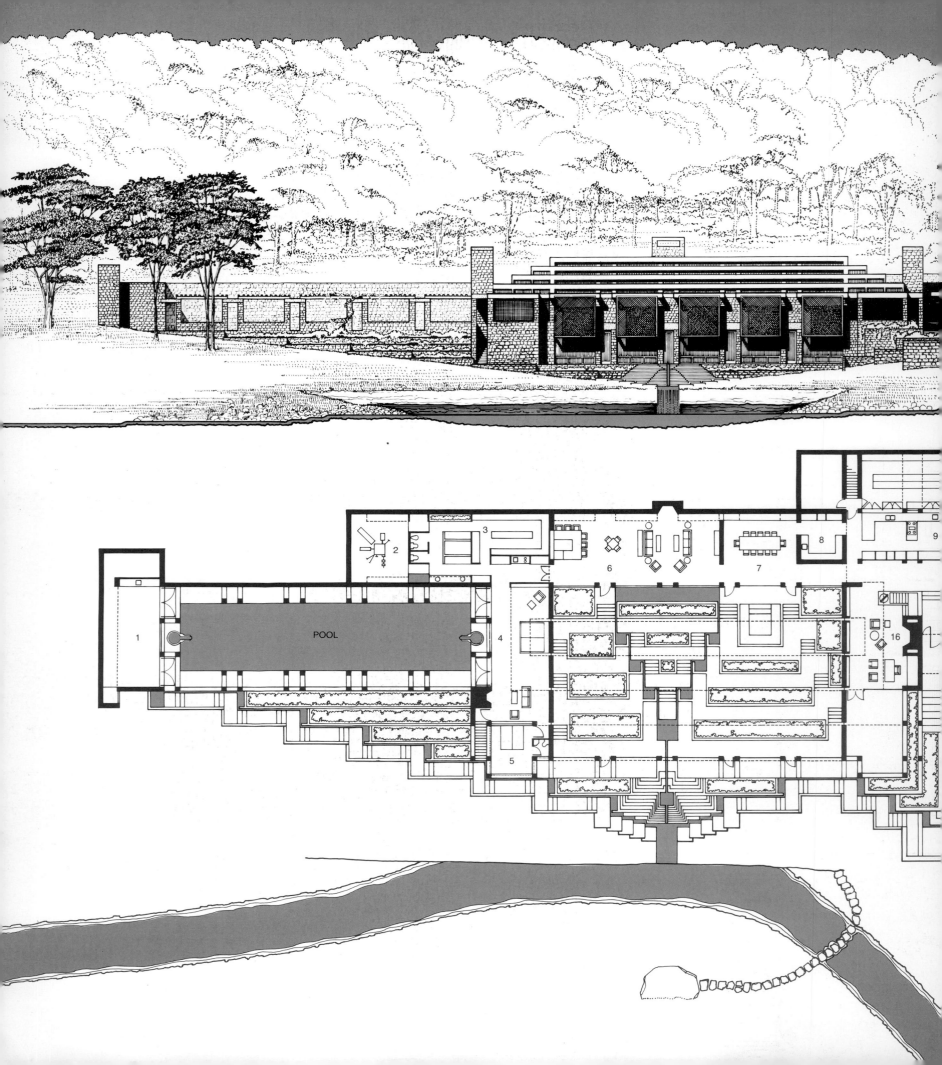

POOL

1

2

3

4

5

6

7

8

9

16

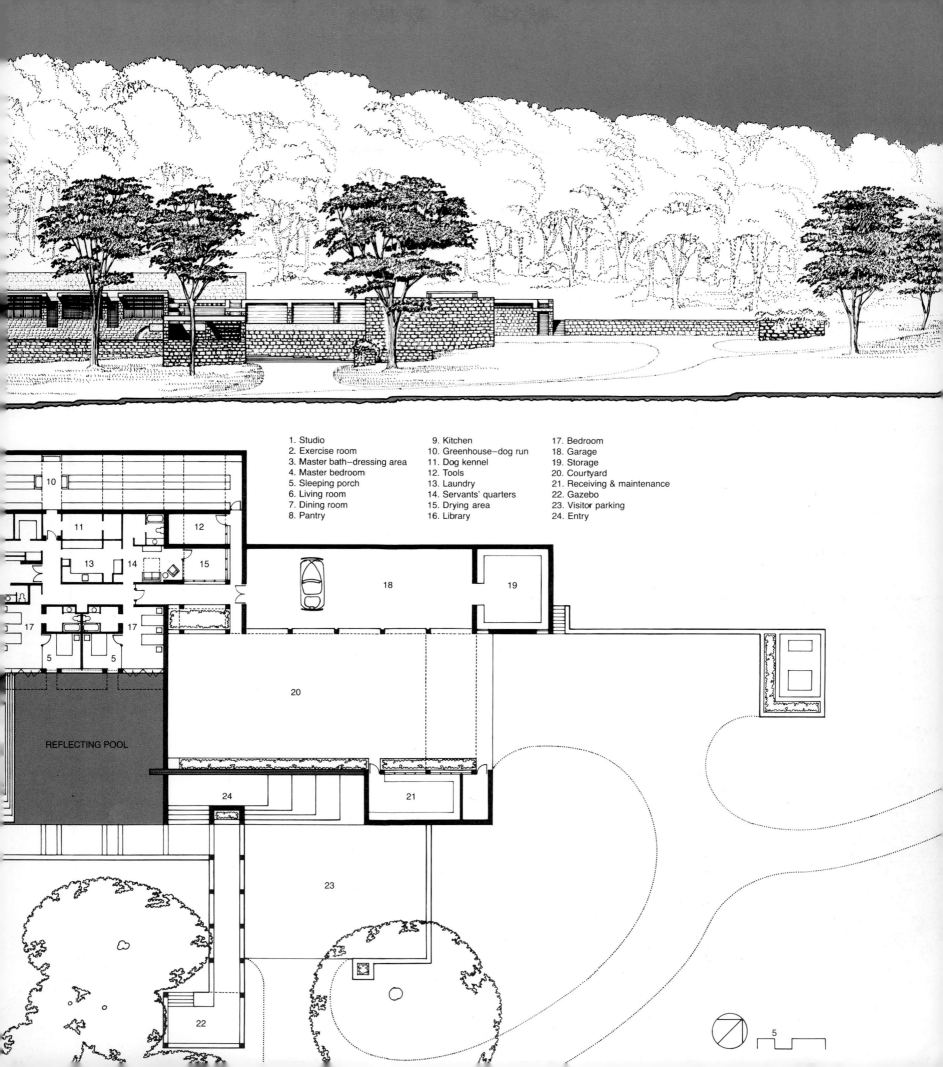

1. Studio
2. Exercise room
3. Master bath–dressing area
4. Master bedroom
5. Sleeping porch
6. Living room
7. Dining room
8. Pantry
9. Kitchen
10. Greenhouse–dog run
11. Dog kennel
12. Tools
13. Laundry
14. Servants' quarters
15. Drying area
16. Library
17. Bedroom
18. Garage
19. Storage
20. Courtyard
21. Receiving & maintenance
22. Gazebo
23. Visitor parking
24. Entry

REFLECTING POOL

5

# MESA HOUSING

*Austin, Texas, 1982–1984*

Three residences for Creek House ranch employees and their families were also designed in 1982. The site had a 1:15 slope to the north. A highway bordered the site to the northeast.

The three houses, each square in plan—32' × 32', were to be placed on an earth terrace. Each was surrounded by an earth berm—64' × 64' overall—and would have a pyramid-shaped roof.

Each house would have had two bedrooms, a shared bath, and a kitchen, dining area, and living area. Parking for ten cars would be provided in a common area.

The site plan for this group of three houses utilized seven squares. It was decided to build the houses on another site, the first site being too close to the highway. The second plan was a circular configuration to be built in two phases—three houses in the first phase and the possibility of two "infills" in a second phase. The first three houses were built.

A variant of this design had been proposed in 1979 as a linear configuration for transient staff housing for the Okefenokee National Wildlife Refuge in Georgia. The interior floor plan was somewhat different.

CLIENT: *Mr. and Mrs. Richardson B. Gill*

ORIGINAL SITE PLAN

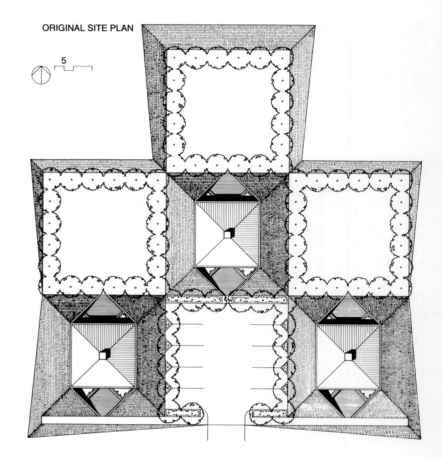

5

PLAN FOR OKEFENOKEE NATIONAL WILDLIFE REFUGE

5

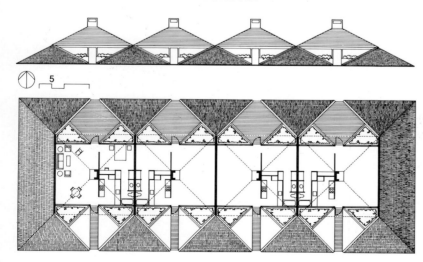

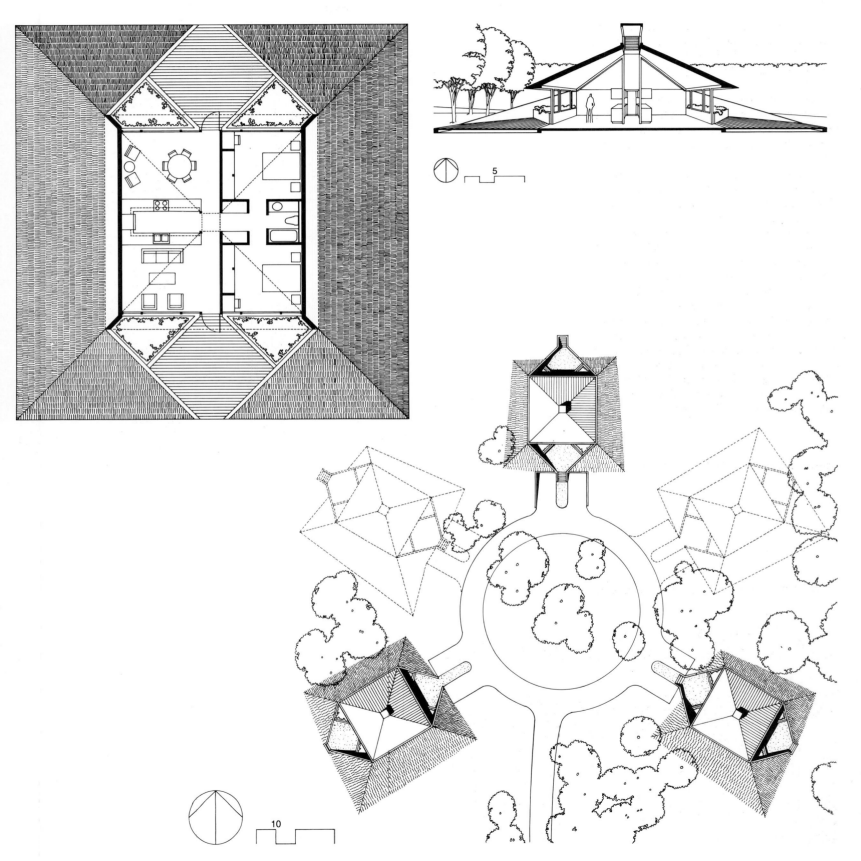

5

10

# ASSESSMENT

William Morgan's architectural commissions in this period tended to be large projects for corporate clients.

The Neiman-Marcus department store in Fort Lauderdale was an unusual commission in that Morgan was the architect of the "shell" of this building. Other specialists designed such elements as lighting and interior furnishings. Morgan's assignment was to design a containing form that would be functional, accessible, and, most important, visually identifiable. The latter was a condition of the siting of this structure amidst the general visual cacophony if not anomie of the automobile-oriented shopping center environment. Morgan acknowledges the massing system of the Karl Liebknecht and Rosa Luxemburg memorials in Berlin, designed by Miës van der Rohe (1926) as a source of his system of articulated massing.

The three electric substation designs are direct products of the problems they attempted to answer, but Morgan acknowledges three designs as references. One is the Sapelo shell rings in Sapelo Island, Georgia (ca. 1700 B.C.). A second is the U.S. Embassy for Amman, Jordan, designed by Paul Rudolph (1956). A third is the roof system of the U.S. Consulate in Luanda, Angola, designed by Louis Kahn (1959–1962).

The Westinghouse Headquarters makes use of the paired-beam structural system, following the development of this system in three major buildings completed earlier. The building is one of Morgan's most successful in its handling of interior light.

The EDS Headquarters building, not realized, could have been a great contribution to those essays in architecture that introduce works of distinct form at large scale into large natural landscape settings, in this case the near-flat plains of North Texas.

The Scheininger Clinic stands as still another successful exercise in burrowing a building into the earth. The circular corner light courts may be considered in relation to the "light cylinders" proposed in the unfortunately unrealized design by Louis Kahn for a synagogue alongside Independence Mall in Philadelphia (1961–1970).

The Creek House, one of Morgan's most lavish projects, suggests some interesting horizons in itself and in relation to Morgan's work. In order to study Spanish American colonial site planning and architecture, Mr. Gill and Morgan flew to Granada, Spain, to visit the Alhambra and to Presidio, Texas, the site of historic Fort Leaton in the Big Bend area overlooking the Rio Grande, and Mexico beyond.

The clients planned to conduct seminars in the Creek House. They are interested in many fields, some of which they actively support. Their interests include a new astronomical laboratory for the University of Texas, real estate development, creative arts of the Texas Hill Country, pre-Columbian archaeology, and broadening and raising the standards for higher education in Texas. Mr. Gill's background is primarily in banking and oil. The Gills are also involved in international diplomacy. The dining room was therefore designed to accommodate ambassadors and chiefs of state. The Gills have traveled in Latin America, Europe, and the Middle East. The house was designed to be animated by its owners' guests.

As for its relation to the body of Morgan's work, this project stands in marked contrast in a special sense. Much of Morgan's residential work derives from an interest in providing compact sheltering interior space in an often vast—and respected—natural setting. (His childhood recollection of the below-decks area of a sailboat in contrast to the scale of the vast seascape-skyscape comes to mind.) With the Creek House a new relationship of domestic-natural spaces was explored.

An interesting by-product of this project was the design of houses for ranch employees. The old scale and spatial relationship was recalled. This design was an application of a project to provide residences for transient staff in the Okefenokee Wildlife Refuge in 1979.

Morgan's design for the Creek House drew largely on premises of the Alhambra, but it also drew reference from the garden designs of the Mexican architect Luis Barragán, particularly his design for Los Clubes in Mexico City (1963–1964). However one might compare the Creek House to Morgan's previous work, it does demonstrate considerable promise for exploration in newer directions, ones that it is hoped can be pursued in future work.

In 1983, after seventeen years of work, Morgan had the time and resources to augment his earlier global travels. He spent a month in Micronesia, returning after thirty years to the prehistoric sites that had come to his attention while he was in the U.S. Navy and whose study had been encouraged by Sigfried Gideon. Morgan visited the little-known prehistoric sites of Pohnpei, Kosrae, Yap, Palau, Guam, and Rota. His investigations have included special focus on the ancient stone cities of Nan Madol and Leluh, the traditional villages of Bechiyal and Irrai, the stone-columned *latte* houses of the Marianas, and the megalithic sculptures and terraced hills of Palau. His studies will be published in *Prehistoric Architecture in Micronesia* (University of Texas Press, 1988).

BLOOMINGDALE'S

GILLDORN SAVINGS

TEN CENTRAL PARK

SUBMARINE BASE HEADQUARTERS

BAPTIST MEDICAL PAVILION

LAW EXCHANGE

BEACH UNITED METHODIST CHURCH

1982—1986

# BLOOMINGDALE'S

*Miami, Florida, 1982–1984*

The Bloomingdale's department store building is located in a shopping mall. To its east is a three-story parking garage, to its west an array of one-story buildings forming a linear landscaped space. This space has a meandering linear pool. A stream borders the southern part of the site; surface parking is on the north.

The building is based on a 32′ × 32′ structural bay. It is seven bays wide (east-west) and eleven bays long (north-south). The building measures 227′ × 344′ and contains 225,000 sf of space, all above grade.

It has three customer entrances—on the north, east, and west sides, at their centers. The west entrance is from the landscaped mall. The south entrance is for truck service.

At the center of the building is a three-story-high atrium with escalators. Near each corner are emergency exit stairs, in towers articulated on the exterior.

The building exterior is treated as a series of rectilinear masses, some forming landscaped terraces. Floors are cantilevered to achieve this treatment, which creates a striking sun-and-shadow composition, asserting the building's presence in the landscape. It also establishes a harmonizing scale with the one-story wood building of the mall. A projecting element casts a shadow over the west (mall) entrance, contributing an effective portal termination for the mall.

In addition to these features, this building makes a particular contribution to the age-old challenge of the architectural treatment of "turning" a building's corners. This building poses a powerful answer.

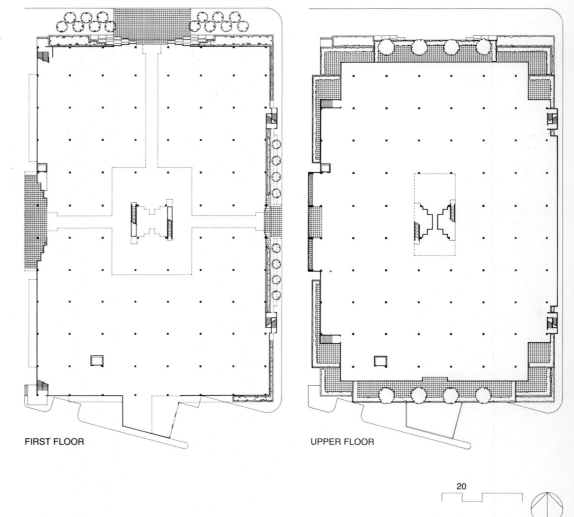

FIRST FLOOR

UPPER FLOOR

20

CLIENT: *Bloomingdale's*
STRUCTURAL, MECHANICAL, AND ELECTRICAL
ENGINEER: *H. J. Ross Associates*
LANDSCAPE ARCHITECT: *Stressau, Smith, and Stressau*
INTERIOR DESIGN: *Hambrecht-Terrell International*
LIGHTING: *William Lam Associates*
CONTRACTOR: *Kroll Construction Co.*

# GILLDORN SAVINGS
*Mt. Zion, Illinois, 1982–1984*

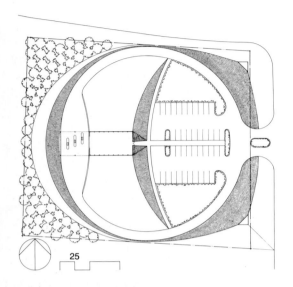

25

The Gilldorn Savings Association commissioned Morgan to design two savings and loan banking facilities. Both were designed to reduce heat gain or loss, to make maximum use of natural daylight, and to provide space for community activities. The Mt. Zion bank is shown here.

The use of earth berms aided in reducing energy consumption while recalling the ancient forms of Indian earth sculptures built in the Ohio Valley between 500 B.C. and A.D. 200 and in Illinois between A.D. 900 and 1200.

The structure has two floors, the lower one being a community room. The upper floor has a banking room, conference room, and office.

CLIENT: *Gilldorn Savings Association*
STRUCTURAL ENGINEER: *M. Dean Worth*
MECHANICAL AND ELECTRICAL ENGINEER: *Hall-Schwartz and Associates*
CIVIL ENGINEER: *Phillip W. Cochran*
INTERIOR DESIGN: *Omniplan Architects*
ACOUSTICS: *Lyle Yerges*
GRAPHIC DESIGN: *Lippincott and Margulies*
CONTRACTORS: *Fisher-Stoune, Inc., and Harold O'Shea Builders*

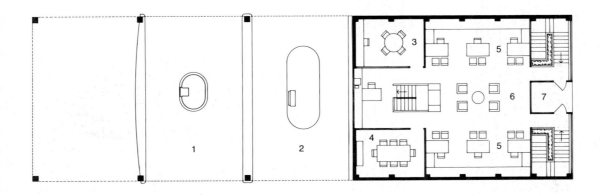

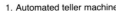

1. Automated teller machine
2. Drive-in tellers
3. Office
4. Conference
5. Banking
6. Waiting
7. Porch
8. Community room

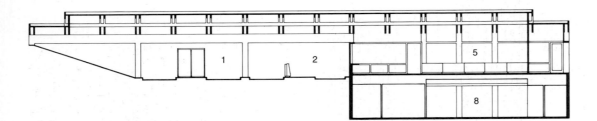

# TEN CENTRAL PARK

*Stuart, Florida, 1982–1983*

This project began with the development of a master site plan that would accommodate two four-story speculative office buildings and four two-story buildings. One of the four-story buildings has been completed and is illustrated here.

The taller buildings have 40,000 square feet each, the lower buildings were planned for a total of 34,000 sf. Surface parking was to be provided at a ratio of 5.5 cars per 1,000 net sf of building area.

The owner's budget specified a cost of $46 / sf, excluding tenant finishes, land cost, and fees.

The site plan proposed a bermed lagoon for each of the taller buildings. The four lower buildings would be arranged around a land-scaped interior court. From the adjoining highway the inward views would be enhanced by the lagoons and berms, the berms screening the sight of the surface-parked cars.

For the four-story building a central service core occupies one of nine square structural modules. A system of four pinwheel rectangular structural segments cantilevers outward at its ends to create a bold architectural identification. All this has been achieved with a rather modest budget.

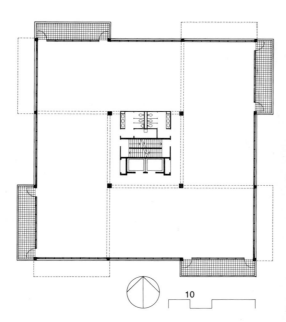

10

CLIENT: *Personal Economics Group of Florida, Inc.*
STRUCTURAL ENGINEER: *H. W. Keister Associates*
MECHANICAL AND ELECTRICAL ENGINEER:
*Roy Turknett Engineers*
CONTRACTOR: *Construction management by owner*

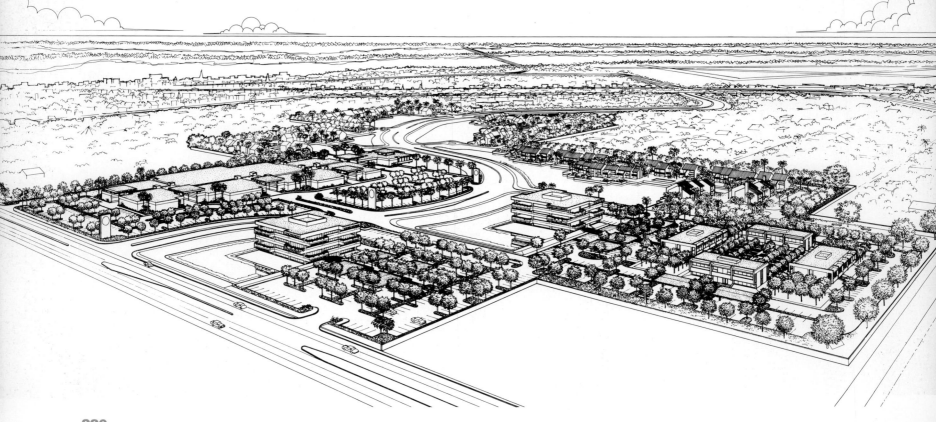

# SUBMARINE BASE HEADQUARTERS

*Kings Bay Naval Base, Camden County, Georgia, 1982–1987*

This building houses three distinct but related functions. It is the headquarters of the commander of a submarine fleet, it is the headquarters of the commander of a naval base, and it is a communications center for the fleet it serves.

The communications center is used by both commands and had to be readily accessible to both. At the same time it was necessary that each command have distinct identity. Naturally, the building had to have a high degree of security.

Two additional factors complicated the program. One was that the accommodations for the commander of the submarine fleet, while requiring identity, constituted only a fifth of the building's area. Second, the building was to be built in two phases, second-phase construction not to interfere with operations.

The first phase consists of the offices of the commander of the base (35,000 gross sf) and the communications center (17,000 gross sf). The second phase will contain the offices of the commander of the submarine fleet (12,500 gross sf). Total building area will be 64,500 gross sf.

The building has the shape of a T in plan. Its northern side has an entrance for the commander of the base. The southern side was designed to rise in the shape of a two-story pyramid, the lower portion being the communications center, the upper the offices of the commander of the submarine fleet. The latter has its distinct entrance on the south side of the building. A service entrance is on the west side.

As an aside, it is interesting to note that a large building is more tolerant of the particular demands of its interior spaces than is a small one.

The building exterior is red brick, with segmented arches at the entrances. This treatment harmonizes with the established architectural character of the area.

Structurally, the building is cast-in-place concrete with a metal superstructure forming the upper pyramid. The roof is corrugated metal, again to harmonize with established architectural character.

Both the elongated and regular pyramid forms of the "bar" and "leg" of the T rise to provide underroof space. Mechanical equipment and antennas are housed there.

The entire building is surrounded by a sloped berm, which is recessed to form landscaped courtyards for portions of the ground floor as well as the upper floor.

The building is served by the Base's cold-and-hot-water system. It has its own emergency mechanical equipment.

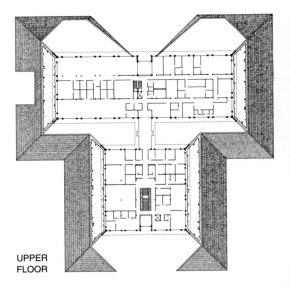

UPPER FLOOR

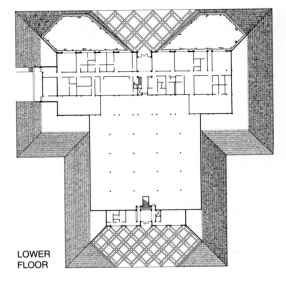

LOWER FLOOR

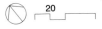

20

CLIENT: *Naval Facilities Engineering Command*
STRUCTURAL ENGINEER: *H. W. Keister Associates*
MECHANICAL AND ELECTRICAL ENGINEER: *Turknett / MPS Engineers*
LANDSCAPE ARCHITECT: *Diversified Environmental Planning*
GRAPHIC DESIGN: *Dave Meyer and Associates*
CONTRACTOR: *Black-Bodenhamer*

# BAPTIST MEDICAL PAVILION

*Jacksonville, Florida, 1983–1986*

This medical building combines a number of related functions best understood by identifying the uses of the various sets of floors.

The ground level has two entrances, one from an automobile "drop off," the other from a large parking garage. The ground floor has commercial shops related to medical treatment.

Floors 2 through 5 accommodate various medical services. Floors 6 and 7 are occupied by a 48-room hotel for visiting ambulatory patients and for patients' families.

Floors 8 through 17, ten floors in all, provide offices for some one hundred physicians and their staffs. Centered on an internal mechanical core, offices are arranged around a double circulation loop. The inner loop (around the core) provides access for patients and visitors. The outer loop (near the building exterior) is for use by physicians and staff.

The building occupies a 204' × 205' site, or 49,200 sf. The structure itself is 115'4" × 115'4". Its seventeen stories reach a height of 216' and contain 278,600 gross sf of floor area. The building is the newest element in a group of buildings that constitute a major medical center.

The structure consists of an inner core, supported on four columns, and eight pairs of exterior columns, which support cantilevered beams. Between the inner core and the perimeter truss is a clear span of 37', allowing a high degree of freedom for interior arrangements.

The paired exterior columns also serve as vertical mechanical chases. This is particularly helpful for a medical building, where mechanical systems are subject to change or addition. Like the column system the chases aid flexibility. On floors where this space is not occupied it can be used as office storage.

The structure is steel frame. The exterior façade is made of glass-fiber-reinforced concrete panels and solar glazing. The protruding spandrels also shade exterior glass.

CLIENT: *Baptist Medical Center*
ASSOCIATED ARCHITECTS: *Falick / Klein Partnership and Drexel Toland Associates*
ENGINEER: *Tilden, Lobnitz, and Cooper, Inc.*
LANDSCAPE ARCHITECT: *Herbert / Halback, Inc.*
INTERIOR DESIGN (PUBLIC SPACES):
*James A. Beaubouef*
CONTRACTOR: *The Auchter Co.*

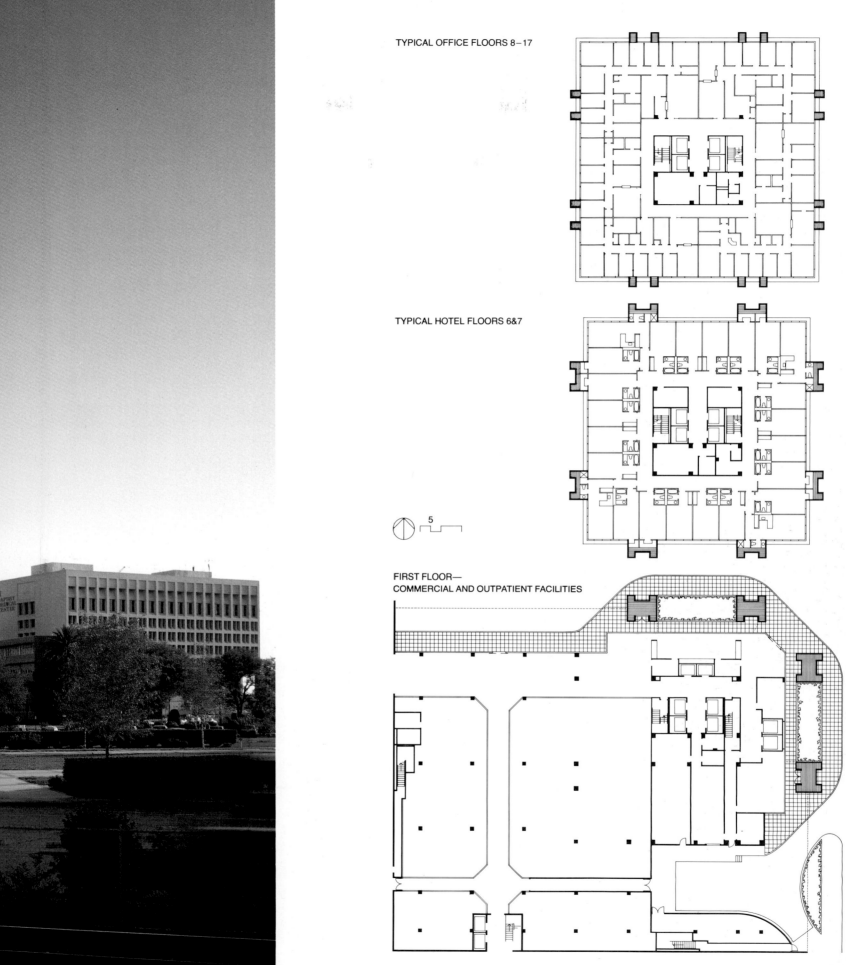

TYPICAL OFFICE FLOORS 8–17

TYPICAL HOTEL FLOORS 6&7

5

FIRST FLOOR—
COMMERCIAL AND OUTPATIENT FACILITIES

# LAW EXCHANGE

*Jacksonville, Florida, 1984–1985*

The Law Exchange building is an excellent example of an architect-developer building done in the right place and with a level of quality not often achieved in speculative office buildings.

Located alongside Morgan's office—itself a development venture of its designer—the Law Exchange is strategically located near four major governmental buildings. These include the Police Administration Building, the County Courthouse and Jail, the City Hall, and the Daniel Building. Two of these were designed by Morgan.

Principally intended for occupancy by lawyers and others whose work is related to government, the building addresses one of the foremost problems of professionals in a downtown area such as this, namely, parking. Occupants as well as their clients have the advantage of an unusually high ratio of parking to office space, namely 2.25 parking spaces per 1,000 net sf of office space.

The building occupies a corner site of 6,349 sf. Its two lower floors are for parking, a total of thirty-seven cars. Each level has a separate entrance to avoid space-wasting interior ramping. Column location and core design do not interfere with efficient car layout.

The entrance lobby of the building is at ground level, the level of the upper parking floor. Above this are three floors of offices, a total of 19,117 gross sf. The fourth and fifth floors have a skylit atrium.

Column layout makes it possible to have two uninterrupted rectangular spaces on each floor, each measuring about 35' × 68'. This allows a number of possible suite configurations for one-person or multiperson professional offices.

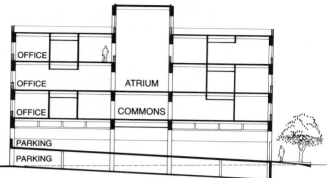

SECTION

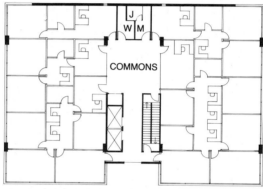

LOWER OFFICE FLOOR

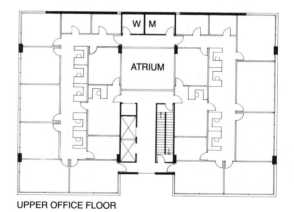

UPPER OFFICE FLOOR

The vertical core contains two passenger elevators, toilet and janitorial rooms, and an ingenious double emergency exit stair, the latter an efficient space saver.

The building has six mechanical zones per floor for energy-use control. It is sprinklered for tenant security. Structure is reinforced concrete. The exterior is cast-in-place finished concrete with infilling concrete masonry units.

The building occupies the site of two predecessors and is a contribution to the support of Jacksonville's downtown redevelopment.

STRUCTURAL ENGINEER: *H. W. Keister Associates*
MECHANICAL AND ELECTRICAL ENGINEER: *Kashmiry and Mahin*
LANDSCAPE ARCHITECT: *Diversified Environmental Planning*
GRAPHIC DESIGN: *Dave Meyer and Associates*
CONTRACTOR: *D. Coleman, Inc.*

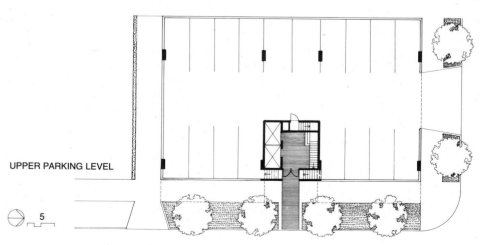

UPPER PARKING LEVEL

5

# BEACH UNITED METHODIST CHURCH
*Jacksonville Beach, Florida, 1985–1987*

Established prior to World War II, this church has been enlarged in several phases. It consists of a worship chapel, Sunday school area, fellowship hall, and administrative offices. All are grouped around an open court. The original building was constructed of local coquina rock, which was extracted from the sea and is now a protected material.

Morgan's design includes a master plan for developing the entire site. This plan would incorporate the existing buildings into a three-courtyard complex. Additional buildings would include a new church as the complex's focal piece, a number of flexible-use classrooms, and a new kitchen for the fellowship hall.

The design draws on numerous forms long associated with religious worship. The dominant form would be the new church building itself, its modified octagonal form rising as a symbolic triangle and culminating in a triangle-form support structure.

Artful use of sheltering colonnades is made in the new courtyards, reminiscent of cloisters. Openness and shelter are a recurring motif. The complex will have four entry points, all welcoming people into tranquil and colonnaded courts.

The church entrance is from two of the courtyards, this experience serving to set a transitional mood. The church interior is arranged at a 45° angle to the complex's general north-south configuration. Its traditional central aisle is on axis with a large northeast-oriented stained-glass window. The aisle serves traditional ceremonial functions. Flanking it at its entrance are two rooms, one for brides, the other for ushers. Side stairs give access to upper-level seating and an organ and choir loft. This upper level is subtly joined to the lower by stairs terminating at the altar.

View lines are open, deployed to reinforce the sense of community among congregants. The interior form and acoustic treatment augment the sound of the choir from the entrance (narthex) as well as the sound of the speaking voice from the pulpit.

The interior volume enlarges toward the altar. Lighting is by means of horizontal clerestories set in the roof's rising plane. The total area of the church is 8,840 sf. There will be seating for six hundred persons.

The project budget is approximately $900,000 for constructing, furnishing, and equipping the church. In a second phase, a bank of new classrooms will be built and the fellowship hall relocated. The budget for this is about $600,000. In a third stage, still more classrooms and other improvements will be made at a cost of about $450,000.

CLIENT: *Beach United Methodist Church*
STRUCTURAL ENGINEER: *H. W. Keister Associates*
MECHANICAL AND ELECTRICAL ENGINEER: *Kashmiry and Mahin*
STAINED-GLASS WINDOWS: *J. Piercey Studios, Inc.*
CONTRACTOR: *Lee and Griffin Construction Co., Inc.*

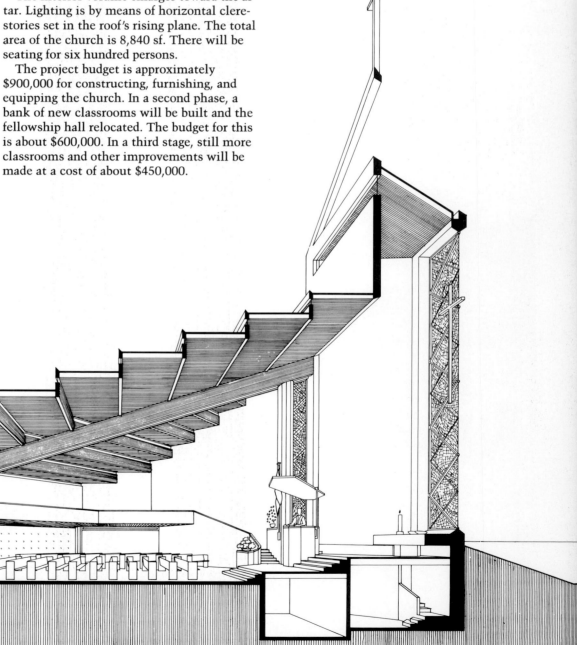

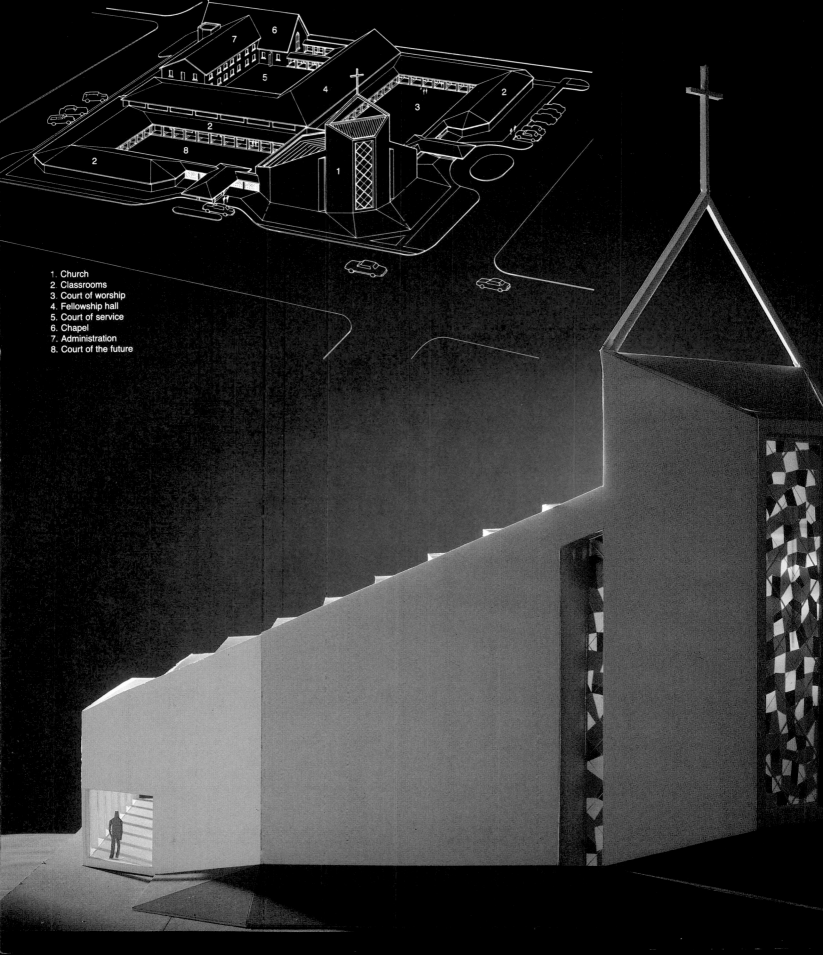

1. Church
2. Classrooms
3. Court of worship
4. Fellowship hall
5. Court of service
6. Chapel
7. Administration
8. Court of the future

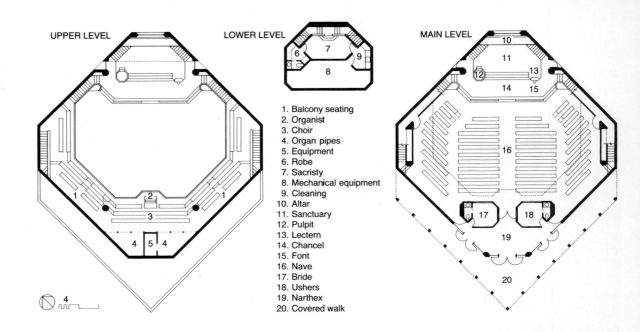

UPPER LEVEL

LOWER LEVEL

MAIN LEVEL

1. Balcony seating
2. Organist
3. Choir
4. Organ pipes
5. Equipment
6. Robe
7. Sacristy
8. Mechanical equipment
9. Cleaning
10. Altar
11. Sanctuary
12. Pulpit
13. Lectern
14. Chancel
15. Font
16. Nave
17. Bride
18. Ushers
19. Narthex
20. Covered walk

# ASSESSMENT

The largest project of Morgan's most recent interval of work was the Baptist Medical Pavilion, for which complex he also prepared a master development plan.

The Medical Pavilion exhibits a skilled integration of structure, mechanical systems, diverse functions, and expressive architectural form.

The Gilldorn Savings banks were modest essays in creating sheltering structures amidst the vast flat plains of the upper Midwest. Morgan notes the well-known Cahokia mounds at Collinsville, Illinois, as a reference (ca. A.D. 900–1200).

In the Ten Central Park speculative office buildings group Morgan has shown how a sense of quality and place can be achieved in an otherwise modest structure.

The Submarine Base Headquarters is both an essay and a test of the validity of earth-pyramid structures. It is a system that, in deft hands, has a high degree of flexibility of size, form, internal arrangements, and use.

The Law Exchange is an essay in making much of a modest project on a modest site. It also demonstrates that speculative architecture can also be architecture of quality.

The Methodist Church is an exercise in both master site planning and architectural expression. Here, again, a modest opportunity has been enlarged to a level of elegance. Particularly noteworthy in this design is the skillful handling of space, light, circulation, and the various constituent parts of the building. They have an integral and fully interdependent flow. Morgan refers to several designs as sources of thought. One is the San Giovanni degli Eremiti in Palermo, Sicily (1142–1148). The second is San Carlo alle Quattro Fontane in Rome, designed by Francesco Borromini (1638–1641). The third is San Lorenzo in Turin, designed by Guarino Guarini (1666–1679).

Reflecting on the qualities that impel his work, Morgan has given considerable thought to the principles that have guided other architects identified with modern architecture. Regarding Frank Lloyd Wright, he has noted that master's utilization of space as a commanding reality, the use of glass, continuity, use of materials, and pattern as ornament. Reflecting on Louis Kahn, he has noted that master's sense of composition, his respect for material, his emphasis on interior space, his use and manipulation of light, and his emphasis on the architectural integration of a building's components. Morgan also acknowledges the influence of Luis Barragán—his simple yet sophisticated use of planes, color, and water. Regarding Le Corbusier, Morgan has examined that master's utilization of pilotis, roof gardens, open plans, continuous fenestration, and the façade as an enveloping skin.

Looking at his own work and the tenets that have guided him, Morgan recognizes five elements. First is the importance of *sense of place*—establishing it where it is not clearly stated or reinforcing it where it is established. Second is *expression of purpose*—that a building should convey through its appearance the purpose it serves. Third is *movement*—the progression and passage of a person in a building. Movement in a building may be thought of as a kind of architectural choreography—linear or curvilinear, straight or angled, rapid or slow, dynamic or passive. And movement may cease when arriving at a place of repose.

Fourth is *light*—its play, manipulation, reflection, heightening, or diminution. Light reveals space. Architecture does not exist without it. Fifth is the *use of materials* and *the construction system*. The materials selected for a building must be appropriate to the purpose being served. At the same time a building must be readily constructable.

Morgan believes strongly that every urban project should offer something to the public as well as serving the sponsor's needs. Examples include the rooftop amphitheater of the Daniel Building, the rooftop garden of the Police Administration Building, and the plaza of the Federal Courts Building. Were all buildings to have such attributes the livability of our cities would be enhanced considerably.

Morgan also believes in creating an architecture that is readily understandable. All great art must communicate directly with the people who come into contact with it, additional and loftier meanings not precluded. Morgan points to Shakespeare's writing as an example, touching people directly and not requiring explanation. Morgan would add a touch of landscape, a bench, a fountain, a portico, or a special detail of unexpected delight—but a familiar one. Such an approach to architecture has no need for (or indeed place for) false arches, fashionable colors, trendy details, or abstruse allusions.

Though simply stated as principles, these guiding thoughts are but points of departure for Morgan's explorations in architecture.

*Florida Architect*, July/August 1971, pp. 31–32.
*Cembureau* (Paris), July 1972, pp. xiii, xiv.
*Campus Buildings That Work*. Philadelphia: North American Publishing Co., 1972, pp. 162–164.
*l'Architecture d'Aujourd'hui* (Paris), September/October 1973, p. xxxv.
*Journal of the American Institute of Architects*, February 1974, pp. 32–39.
*L'Industria delle Costruzioni* (Rome), April 1974, pp. 5–15.
*L'Industria Italiana del Cemento* (Rome), March 1976, pp. 163–176.
*Japan Architect* (Tokyo), October 1977.
*Progressive Architecture*, April 1979, p. 86.
*Interiors*, October 1980, p. 75.
*Architecture, 1970–1980: A Decade of Change*, by Jeanne M. Davern. New York: McGraw-Hill, 1980, pp. 36–37.
*Process: Architecture* (Tokyo), #21, January 1981, p. 124.
*The Architecture of the United States: Vol. 2, The South and Mid-West*, by G. E. Kidder Smith. New York: Anchor Press/Doubleday, 1981, pp. 37–39.
*Earth Shelters*, by David Martindale. New York: E. P. Dutton, 1981, pp. 66–67.
*Fifty Outstanding Architects of the World*, by Ivica Mladjenović. Reprint, Belgrade: Izgradnja, 1984, pp. 51, 53.

Stanley Residence
*Architectural Record*, September 1971, pp. 135–139.
*House and Home*, June 1972, pp. 80, 89.
*Florida Architect*, July 1972, pp. 23–25.
*Architecture + Urbanism* (Tokyo), September 1972, p. 108.
*Informes de la Construcción* (Madrid), November 1975, pp. 25–29.

Amelia Island Dunehouses
*Washington Post*, 8 April 1972, "Cityscape," by Wolf von Eckardt.
*Architectural Record*, September 1972, p. 136.
*Journal of the American Institute of Architects*, February 1974, pp. 32–39.
*Florida Architect*, May/June 1975, cover, pp. 6–11.
*Bauen und Wohnen* (Zurich), June 1977, p. 302.

Morgan Residence
*Architectural Record*, September 1972, p. 132; May 1974, p. 39.

*Florida Architect*, September/October 1973, pp. 20, 21.
*House and Garden*, December 1973, pp. 84–89; November 1975, pp. 118–119.
*Journal of the American Institute of Architects*, May 1974, p. 46.
*New York Times*, 2 June 1974.
*Christian Science Monitor*, 9 August 1974, p. 13.
*Architectural Record Houses*, mid-May 1974, pp. 64–67.
*Houses Architects Design for Themselves*, edited by Walter F. Wagner, Jr., and Karin Schlegel. New York: McGraw-Hill, 1974, pp. 104–107.
*World Book Yearbook*. Chicago: Field Enterprises Educational Corporation, 1974, p. 200.
*House and Garden Building Guide*, Spring/Summer 1975, pp. 73–79.
*Bauen und Wohnen* (Zurich), September 1975, pp. 352–353.
*Playboy*, August 1976, pp. 131–133, 149.
*Great Houses*, edited by Walter F. Wagner, Jr. New York: McGraw-Hill, 1976, pp. 32–35.
*Interior Design*, January 1977, pp. 128–135.
*Japan Architect* (Tokyo), October 1977.
*Houses Architects Live In*, by Barbara Plumb. New York: Viking Press, 1977, pp. 124–127.
*Architecture + Urbanism* (Tokyo), September 1978, pp. 133–140.
*Hill Housing*, by Derek Abbott and Kimball Pollit. New York: Watson-Guptill, 1980, p. 89.
*Guide to U.S. Architecture: 1940–1980*, by Esther McCoy and Barbara Goldstein. Santa Monica, Calif.: Arts + Architecture Press, 1982, p. 75.
*Wohnen unter Schrägen Dach*, by A. Mutsch-Engel. Stuttgart: Verlagsanstalt Alexander Koch, 1982, pp. 106, 108.
*Toshi-Jukatu* (Tokyo), August 1983, pp. 38–41.

Pyramid Condominiums
*Architectural Record*, September 1972, pp. 134–135.
*Progressive Architecture*, May 1973, p. 42; January 1975, p. 62; September 1976, pp. 64–67.
*Architecture + Urbanism* (Tokyo), September 1977, pp. 37–48.
*l'Architecture d'Aujourd'hui* (Paris), November 1977, p. xlviii.
*L'Industria delle Costruzioni* (Rome), March 1979, pp. 54–60.

*Transformations in Modern Architecture*, by Arthur Drexler. New York: Museum of Modern Art, 1979, p. 126.

*Housing*, by John Macsai. New York: John Wiley & Sons, 1982, pp. 404, 405.

*Fifty Outstanding Architects of the World*, by Ivica Mladjenović. Reprint, Belgrade: Izgradnja, 1984, pp. 52–53.

Police Administration Building
*Journal of the Institute of American Architects*, May 1972, p. 10.
*Progressive Architecture*, July 1972, p. 24.
*Architectural Record*, September 1972, pp. 129–131.
*Perception and Lighting as Form Givers for Architecture*, by William M. C. Lam. New York: McGraw-Hill, 1977, pp. 260–261.
*Architecture + Urbanism* (Tokyo), June 1978, pp. 53–60.
*Nikkei Architecture* (Tokyo), July 1978, pp. 60–64.
*Design Competitions*, by Paul D. Spreiregen. New York: McGraw-Hill, 1979, pp. 37–43.
*Interiors*, October 1980, p. 75.
*Architecture, 1970–1980: A Decade of Change*, by Jeanne M. Davern. New York: McGraw-Hill, 1980, pp. 204–205.
*Architecture Graphics Textbook*, by Rendow Yee. San Francisco: City College of San Francisco, 1980, p. 94c.
*Institutional Buildings: Architecture for the Controlled Environment*, edited by Louis G. Redstone. New York: McGraw-Hill, 1980, pp. 78–85.
*The Architecture of the United States: Vol. 2, The South and Mid-West*, by G. E. Kidder Smith. New York: Anchor Press/Doubleday, 1981, pp. 41–43.
*Public Art: New Directions*, by Louis G. Redstone. New York: McGraw-Hill, 1981, p. 25.
*Guide to U.S. Architecture: 1940–1980*, by Esther McCoy and Barbara Goldstein. Santa Monica, Calif.: Arts + Architecture Press, 1982, p. 75.
*Fifty Outstanding Architects of the World*, by Ivica Mladjenović. Reprint, Belgrade: Izgradnja, 1984, pp. 53–54.

Memphis Riverfront Development
*Journal of the American Institute of Architects*, February 1974, pp. 32–33.
*Progressive Architecture*, June 1975, p. 36.

Morgan Office Building
*Florida Architect*, September/October 1973, p. 23.

*Architectural Record*, April 1975, p. 98.
*Interior Design*, January 1977, pp. 128–135.
*Decorative Arts and Modern Interiors*, 1978 Annual (London), pp. 64–67.

Hilltop House
*Architectural Record*, September 1972, p. 133.
*Nikkei Architecture* (Tokyo), August 1976, pp. 32–33.
*Newsweek*, 4 October 1976, pp. 66–69.
*Toshi-Jukatu* (Tokyo), November 1976, pp. 21–24.
*Architectural Record Houses of 1976*, pp. 106–107.
*1977 Colliers Year Book Covering the Year 1976*. New York: Macmillan Educational Company, 1976, p. 139.
*Bauen und Wohnen* (Zurich), June 1977, p. 203.
*Architecture + Urbanism* (Tokyo), September 1977, pp. 101–108.
*Der Spiegel* (Munich), 10 October 1977, pp. 254, 255.
*Panorama* (Milan), 20 December 1977, p. 99.
*Journal of the American Institute of Architects*, April 1978, pp. 40–41.
*Transformations in Modern Architecture*, by Arthur Drexler. New York: Museum of Modern Art, 1979, p. 130.
*Architecture, 1970–1980: A Decade of Change*, by Jeanne M. Davern. New York: McGraw-Hill, 1980, p. 162.
*L'Architettura della Caverna*, by Manfredi G. Nicoletti. Rome: Laterza and Figli, 1980, p. 50.
*Process: Architecture* (Tokyo), #21, January 1981, pp. 126–130.
*Maisons creusées maisons enterrées*, by Nichole Charneau and Jean-Charles Trebbi. Paris, 1981, p. 190.
*Stern* (Hamburg), 23 September 1982, pp. 198–204.
*The Handbook of Earth Shelter Design*, by Mike Edelhart. New York: Doubleday, 1982, p. 8.
*Decormag* (Montreal), February 1984, pp. 56–57.
*La Maison de Marie Claire* (Paris), June 1984, pp. 12–13.
*Saturday Review*, September/October 1985, p. 22.
*Geomorphic Architecture*, by Edmund Burger. New York: Van Nostrand Reinhold, 1986, pp. 133–135.

Interama Amphitheater
*Architectural Record*, September 1972, p. 133; February 1975, pp. 81–88.
*Florida Architect*, May/June 1975, pp. 9–10.

Dickinson Residence
*Interiors*, February 1975, pp. 101–102, 139.
*Florida Architect*, May/June 1975, pp. 10–11.

Atlantic Beach Dunehouses
*House and Garden*, April 1976, pp. 122–124; Fall/Winter, pp. 64–67.
*Florida Architect*, September/October 1976, p. 31.
*Interior Design*, January 1977, pp. 128–131.
*Playboy*, February 1977, p. 193.
*Popular Mechanics*, March 1977, pp. 78–81.
*Bauen und Wohnen* (Zurich), June 1977, p. 203.
*Architectural Record*, mid-August 1977, pp. 74–75.
*Der Spiegel* (Munich), 10 October 1977, pp. 254–255.
*Panorama* (Milan), 20 December 1977, p. 99.
*Australian House and Garden* (Melbourne), December 1977.
*Belle* (Sydney), January/February 1978, pp. 94–97.
*Journal of the American Institute of Architects*, April 1978, pp. 38–39.
*Progressive Architecture*, May 1978, pp. 108–109; April 1979, p. 87.
*Newsweek*, 5 June 1978, p. 106.
*Casa Vogue* (Milan), December 1978, pp. 172–175.
*Solar Houses*, by Louis Gropp. New York: Pantheon Books, 1978, pp. 104–105.
*Architecture + Urbanism* (Tokyo), February 1979, pp. 157–159.
*Smithsonian Magazine*, February 1979, pp. 96–105.
*Maison et Jardin* (Paris), June 1979, pp. 112–115.
*National Geographic World*, September 1979, p. 16.
*George Nelson on Design*. New York: Watson-Guptill, 1979.
*Decorative Arts and Modern Interiors* (London), 1979, pp. 22–27; (Paris), 1981, cover, pp. 22–27.
*Transformations in Modern Architecture*, by Arthur Drexler. New York: Museum of Modern Art, 1979, p. 131.
*Somos* (Buenos Aires), 27 June 1980, pp. 52–53.
*Interiors*, October 1980, p. 75.

*House Beautiful*, November/December 1980, p. 106.

*L'Architettura della Caverna*, by Manfredi G. Nicoletti. Rome: Laterza and Figli, 1980, pp. 50, 90.

*The Earth Shelter Handbook*, by Tri/Arch Associates. Milwaukee: Tech/Data Publications, 1980, pp. 178–182.

*Energy-Efficient Buildings*, by Walter F. Wagner, Jr. New York: McGraw-Hill, 1980.

*L'Industria Italiana del Cemento* (Rome), May 1981, pp. 345–354.

*Earth Shelters*, by David Martindale. New York: E. P. Dutton, 1981, jacket.

*Klimagerechte und Energie Sparende Architektur* (Karlsruhe), 1981, pp. 66–67.

*Maisons creusées maisons enterrées*, by Nichole Charneau and Jean-Charles Trebbi. Paris, 1981, p. 181.

*Stern* (Hamburg), 28 September 1982, pp. 198–204.

*Guide to U.S. Architecture: 1940–1980*, by Esther McCoy and Barbara Goldstein. Santa Monica, Calif.: Arts + Architecture Press, 1982, p. 74.

*Earth Sheltered Habitat*, by Gideon S. Golany. New York: Van Nostrand Reinhold, 1983, pp. 29, 36–37.

*Modern Gardens and the Landscape*, by Elizabeth Kassler. New York: Museum of Modern Art, 1984, p. 109.

*Geomorphic Architecture*, by Edmund Burger. New York: Van Nostrand Reinhold, 1986, pp. 124–130.

Perdue Office Building
*Journal of the American Institute of Architects*, February 1974, pp. 32–39.

Beach House
*Florida Architect*, May/June 1975, pp. 10–11.
*Architectural Record*, mid-May 1977, pp. 106–108.
*Nikkei Architect* (Tokyo), August 1977, pp. 50, 51.
*Panorama* (Milan), 20 December 1977, p. 99.
*Record Houses and Apartments.* New York: McGraw-Hill, 1977.
*House Beautiful Building Manual*, Spring/Summer 1978, pp. 88–91.
*Casa Vogue* (Milan), May 1979, pp. 162–167.
*Decormag* (Montreal), February 1984, pp. 52–53.
*La Maison de Marie Claire* (Paris), June 1984, pp. 10–11.

Daniel Building
*Progressive Architecture*, July 1977, p. 40.
*Architectural Record*, January 1978, p. 124.
*Building Design and Construction*, August 1979, pp. 98–102.
*Architecture + Urbanism* (Tokyo), May 1980, pp. 91–97.
*Interiors*, October 1980, p. 75.
*The Architecture of the United States: Vol. 2, The South and Mid-West*, by G. E. Kidder Smith. New York: Anchor Press/Doubleday, 1981, pp. 43–44.
*L'Industria delle Costruzioni* (Rome), October 1983, pp. 50–53.
*Florida Designers Quarterly South*, January 1985, pp. 20–21.

Federal Building, United States Courthouse
*Architectural Record*, December 1978, pp. 116–117; October 1979, pp. 81–86.
*Building Design and Construction*, October 1979, pp. 92–93.
*Architecture + Urbanism* (Tokyo), May 1980, pp. 83–90.
*Journal of the American Institute of Architects*, mid-May 1980, pp. 162–164.
*Institutional Buildings: Architecture for the Controlled Environment.* New York: McGraw-Hill, 1980, pp. 74–75.
*L'Industria delle Costruzioni* (Rome), January 1981, cover, pp. 50–57.
*The Architecture of the United States: Vol. 2, The South and Mid-West*, by G. E. Kidder Smith. New York: Anchor Press/Doubleday, 1981, pp. 36–37.
*Guide to U.S. Architecture: 1940–1980*, by Esther McCoy and Barbara Goldstein. Santa Monica, Calif.: Arts + Architecture Press, 1982, p. 75.
*Fifty Outstanding Architects of the World*, by Ivica Mladjenović. Reprint, Belgrade: Izgradnja, 1984, p. 51.
*Masonry in Architecture*, by Louis G. Redstone. New York: McGraw-Hill, 1984, pp. 40, 41.
*L'Industria Italiana del Cemento* (Rome), June 1986, pp. 522–535.
*Betons* (Paris), December 1986, p. 1.

Sea Gardens
*Architectural Record*, mid-May 1979, pp. 122–123.
*Toshi-Jukatu* (Tokyo), November 1979, pp. 24–27.
*Process: Architecture* (Tokyo), #12, 1980, pp. 130–135.

*L'Industria delle Costruzioni* (Rome), September 1981, pp. 44–48.
*Housing*, by John Macsai. New York: John Wiley & Sons, 1982, p. 488.

Watkins Residence
*Architecture + Urbanism* (Tokyo), July 1980, p. 48.

Florida State Conference Center
*Architecture + Urbanism* (Tokyo), August 1983, pp. 102–108.
*Florida Architect*, July/August 1985, pp. 22–24.

Forest House
*Progressive Architecture*, April 1979, pp. 84–87.
*Architectural Digest*, December 1979, pp. 86–93.
*Architectural Record*, mid-May 1980, pp. 114–116.
*Architecture + Urbanism* (Tokyo), July 1980, pp. 51–54.
*Interiors*, October 1980, pp. 74–75.
*Toshi-Jukatu* (Tokyo), December 1980, cover, pp. 32–35.
*Process: Architecture* (Tokyo), #21, 1981, cover, pp. 131–137.
*Earth Shelters*, by David Martindale. New York: E. P. Dutton, 1981, pp. 126–127.
*Architectural Digest, Le Pui Belle Casa del Mondo* (Rome), April 1983, pp. 98–103.
*Decormag* (Montreal), February 1984, pp. 54–55.
*La Maison de Marie Claire* (Paris), June 1984, pp. 14–15.
*Geomorphic Architecture*, by Edmund Burger. New York: Van Nostrand Reinhold, 1986, pp. 136–138.

District Court of Appeal, First District
*Florida Bar Journal*, January 1981, pp. 8–10.
*Architectural Record*, January 1983, pp. 116–121.
*Architecture + Urbanism* (Tokyo), August 1983, pp. 91–98.
*Florida Architect*, Fall 1983, p. 30.
*L'Industria delle Costruzioni* (Rome), June 1984, pp. 50–56.

Oceanfront Townhouses
*Florida Architect*, Fall 1982, p. 13.
*Architecture + Urbanism*, April 1983, pp. 54–57.

Treehouse
*Florida Architect*, Fall 1983, p. 29.
*New Shelter*, July/August 1985, p. 102.

Westinghouse Headquarters
*Orlando Magazine*, February 1984, pp. 78–80.
*Corporate Design*, September/October 1984,
  pp. 132–133.
*Corporate Design and Realty*, November/
  December 1984, cover, pp. 51–57.
*Architectural Record*, August 1985,
  pp. 100–104.
*L'Industria delle Costruzioni* (Rome), January
  1987, pp. 42–47.

Scheininger Clinic
*Architecture + Urbanism* (Tokyo), April
  1983, pp. 58–59.
*Architecture*, August 1985, pp. 74–75.

Creek House
*Florida Architect*, September/October 1984,
  pp. 42–43.

Bloomingdale's
*Florida Architect*, May/June 1986, pp. 22–27.
*Interior Design*, February 1987, pp. 272–275.

Gilldorn Savings
*Corporate Design*, October/November 1984,
  p. 133.
*Florida Architect*, November/December 1984,
  p. 35.
*Architecture*, February 1985, pp. 82–83.
*Interior Design*, August 1985, pp. 220–223.

General
*Contemporary Architects*, edited by Muriel
  Emanuel. New York: St. Martin's Press,
  1980, pp. 561–563.
*Macmillan Encyclopedia of Architects*, edited
  by Adolf K. Placzek. New York: Free Press/
  Macmillan Publishing Co., 1982, vol. 3,
  p. 239.

By William Morgan
*Prehistoric Architecture in the Eastern
  United States*. Cambridge, Mass.: MIT
  Press, 1980.
*Prehistoric Architecture in Micronesia*. Aus-
  tin: University of Texas Press, 1988.

# INDEX